Skill Sharpeners 1

SECOND EDITION

Judy DeFilippo
Charles Skidmore

ADDISON-WESLEY PUBLISHING COMPANY

Reading, Massachusetts • Menlo Park, California
New York • Don Mills, Ontario • Wokingham, England
Amsterdam • Bonn • Sydney • Singapore • Tokyo • Madrid • San Juan

Judy DeFilippo is a coordinator of ESL in the Intensive English program at Northeastern University. She is author of *Lifeskills 1* and *2* and *Lifeskills and Citizenship,* and is co-author of *Grammar Plus,* all published by Addison-Wesley.

Charles Skidmore is an ESL teacher at the secondary level in the Boston, Massachusetts, schools and at Boston University's CELOP program. He is co-author of *In Good Company* also published by Addison-Wesley.

A Publication of the World Language Division

Editorial: Talbot Hamlin, Elly Schottman

Production/Manufacturing: James W. Gibbons

Illustrations: Elizabeth Hazelton, Kathleen Todd, publisher's files

Cover design: Marshall Henrichs, Richard Hannus

ISBN 0-201-51325-0

6 7 8 9 10-PO-97 96 95 94 93

Introduction

The *Skill Sharpeners* series has been especially designed for students whose skills in standard English, especially those skills concerned with reading and writing, require strengthening. It is directed both toward students whose first language is not English and toward those who need additional practice in standard English grammar and vocabulary. By introducing basic skills tied to classroom subjects in a simple, easy-to-understand grammatical framework, the series helps to prepare these students for success in regular ("mainstream") academic subjects. By developing and reinforcing school and life survival skills, it helps build student confidence and self esteem.

This second edition of *Skill Sharpeners* not only updates the content of many pages, it also provides increased focus for some of the grammar exercises and adds new emphasis on higher order thinking skills. In addition, there are more content-area readings, more biographies, new opportunities for students to write, and more practice in using formats similar to those of many standardized tests. The central purpose of the series remains the same, however. *Skill Sharpeners* remains dedicated to helping your students sharpen their skills in all facets of English communication.

With English as a Second Language students, *Skill Sharpeners* supplements and complements any basic ESL text or series. With these students and with others, *Skill Sharpeners* can also be used to reteach and reinforce specific skills with which students are having—or have had—difficulty. In addition, it can be used to review and practice grammatical structures and to reinforce, expand, and enrich students' vocabularies.

The grammatical structures in the *Skill Sharpeners* series follow a systematic, small-step progression with many opportunities for practice, review, and reinforcement. Vocabulary and skill instruction is presented in the context of situations and concepts that have an immediate impact on students' daily lives. Themes and subject matter are directly related to curriculum areas. Reading and study skills are stressed in many pages, and writing skills are carefully developed, starting with single words and sentences and building gradually to paragraphs and stories in a structured, controlled composition sequence.

If you are using *Skill Sharpeners* with a basic text or series, you may find that the structural presentation in *Skill Sharpeners* deviates from that in your text. In such a case, you should not expect most of your students to be able actively to use the structures on some pages in speaking or writing. The students should, however, be able to read and respond to the content. Do not be concerned about structural errors during discussion of the material. It is important that students become *actively involved* and *communicating*, however imperfectly, from the very beginning.

Using the *Skill Sharpeners*

Because each page or pair of pages of the *Skill Sharpeners* books is independent and self contained, the series lends itself to great flexibility of use. Teachers may pick and choose pages that fit the needs of particular students, or they may use the pages in sequential order. Most pages are self-explanatory, and all are easy to use, either in class or as homework assignments. Annotations at the bottom of each page identify the skill or skills being developed and suggest ways to prepare for, introduce, and present the exercise(s) on the page. In most cases, oral practice of the material is suggested before the student is asked to complete the page in writing. Teacher demonstration and student involvement and participation help build a foundation for completing the page successfully and learning the skill.

The *Skill Sharpeners* are divided into thematic units. The first unit of each book is introductory. In *Skill Sharpeners 1*, this unit provides exercises to help students say and write their names and addresses and to familiarize them with basic classroom language, school deportment, the names of school areas and school personnel, and number names. In later books of the series, the first unit serves both to review some of the material taught in earlier books and to provide orientation to the series for students coming to it for the first time.

At the end of each of the *Skill Sharpeners* books is a review of vocabulary and an end-of-book test of grammatical and reading skills. The test, largely in multiple-choice format, not only assesses learning of the skills but also provides additional practice for other multiple-choice tests.

The complete Table of Contents in each book identifies the skills developed on each page. A Skills Index at the end of the book lists skills alphabetically by topic and indicates the pages on which they are developed.

Skill Sharpeners invite expansion! We encourage you to use them as a springboard and to add activities and exercises that build on those in the books to fill the needs of your own particular students. Used this way, the *Skill Sharpeners* can significantly help to build the confidence and skills that students need to be successful members of the community and successful achievers in subject-area classrooms.

Contents

UNIT 1   Getting Started

What's Your Name? (*Introducing oneself and others*)   9

Names, Addresses, and Numbers (*Discussing address labels, library cards, ID cards*)   10

Classroom Language (*Understanding classroom commands*)   11

Things to Remember (*Understanding school rules*)   12

Which Way? (*Understanding direction words*)   13

At School (*Naming school locations, reading a map*)   14

People and Places at School (*Naming school personnel and school locations*)   15

Number Names (*Naming numbers 1–10,000*)   16

What Time Is It? (*Telling time on the hour*)   17

Matching Times (*Telling time on the hour*)   18

Where Is It? (*Naming classroom furniture and objects, distinguishing left and right*)   19

Tell When, Tell Where (*Naming the days of the week, using pictures to answer questions*)   20

The Months of the Year (*Reading a calendar, naming the months, understanding before and after*)   21

Reading a Calendar (*Reading a calendar, reporting dates*)   22

May I? (*Asking permission*)   23

Talking About Feelings (*Describing feelings, writing short dialogues*)   24

Class Rules (*Reading rules and information*)   25

UNIT 2   Clothes, Color, and Money

Clothing (*Naming articles of clothing*)   26

What Are They Wearing? (*Discussing clothes, writing descriptions*)   27

Counting American Money (*Counting money, reading and writing prices*)   28

Money Problems (*Understanding math language and money transactions*)   29

Categories (*Classifying, memorizing*)   30

Missing Words (*Recognizing and completing familiar phrases using context clues*)   31

The Four Seasons (*Reading for details, making inferences*)   32

Asking Questions (*Asking and writing wh- questions*)   33

Flags, Countries, and Continents (*Reading to find facts, making a chart to organize information*)   34

UNIT 3   Time and Place

What's the Time? (*Telling time, reading signs*)   35

Barrington Bus Company (*Reading a bus schedule*)   36

In, On, or Under? (*Using prepositions in, on, under, behind, next to, writing a paragraph*)   37

Where Are My Things? (*Using prepositions in, on, under, behind, in front of*)   38

The Surprise Party (*Identifying main idea and details, following directions*)   39

Maps (*Reading a map, using prepositions, giving directions*)   40

Following Directions (*Reading a map, following directions*)   41

The New England States (*Reading a map, reading to find facts, writing a paragraph*)   42

UNIT 4   Describing People

Using the Verb "To Be" (*Reviewing present forms of* to be)   43

Anna Garcia (*Reviewing pronouns and adjectives, writing a description*)   44

Describing People and Things (*Reviewing adjectives and present forms of* to be)   45

Information, Please (*Answering questions with present forms of* to be)   46

Stevie Wonder: Reading a Biography (*Reading a biography, making inferences, writing a paragraph*)   47

Using Capital Letters (*Following rules for capitalization*)   48

Letters to a Friend (*Describing, writing a friendly letter*)   49

What's His Name? (*Identifying main idea and details, writing a paragraph*)   50

Dear Dot (*Reading comprehension, making judgments*)   51

UNIT 5   Food and Drink

Food (*Learning food vocabulary, answering multiple choice questions*)   52

Doing Things (*Recognizing subject pronouns, present progressive tense*)   53

Hamburgers Unlimited! (*Practicing money skills, using a chart*)   54

More Food (*Building vocabulary, classifying*)   55

In the Cafeteria (*Using information to make inferences*)   56

Buying Food (*Building vocabulary, reviewing food vocabulary, classifying*)   57

A or An? (*Using articles* a and an)   58

Questions with "Like" (*Differentiating among uses of* like)   59

Dear Dot (*Reading comprehension, making judgments*)   60

UNIT 6   Families and Homes

Families (*Building vocabulary, answering questions*)   61

Amy's Family (*Building vocabulary, understanding a "family tree" chart*)   62

Mr., Mrs., Miss, and Ms. (*Learning, pronouncing, distinguishing among different name titles*)   63

Where Are They? (*Forming contractions, reviewing prepositions*)   64

Bill's Apartment Building (*Building vocabulary, classifying*)   65

What Are They Doing? (*Practicing the present progressive tense*)   66

Spell-ING (*Learning spelling rules for adding* -ing)   67

The Kent Family at Home (*Present progressive, reviewing vocabulary, answering multiple-choice questions*)   68

Two Families (*Answering true-false-? questions, completing a cloze exercise, writing a paragraph*)   69

Writing Questions (*Asking questions using* to be, *present progressive*)   70

Dear Dot (*Reading comprehension, making judgments*)   71

UNIT 7   Occupations and Nationalities

Occupations (*Building vocabulary, using simple present tense*) **72**
More Occupations (*Building vocabulary, using simple present tense*) **73**
A Working Family (*Building vocabulary, making inferences*) **74**
How Much Do They Make? (*Reading a bar graph, understanding more than, less than*) **75**
Interviewing: Personal Preferences (*Using a chart, writing a paragraph*) **76**
Where Are You From? (*Naming countries and nationalities, completing a chart*) **77**
The Right Career (*Reading for details, making inferences, developing career vocabulary*) **78**
My Country and Yours (*Reading for details, writing an informative essay*) **79**
Dear Dot (*Reading comprehension, making judgments*) **80**

UNIT 8   Going Places, Doing Things

There Is, There Are (There is/are, *asking questions, making negative statements*) **81**
Plurals: More than One (*Learning spelling rules for forming plurals, writing original sentences*) **82**
What's Happening at School Today? (*Present progressive, writing a paragraph*) **83**
Interviewing: This School (There is/are, *interviewing, writing a paragraph*) **84**
Reading a Chart (There is/are, *finding information from a chart*) **85**
Reading a Circle Chart (*Interpreting a circle chart, answering true-false questions, making inferences*) **86**
Quincy Market: Reading for Details (*Reading for details*) **87**
Chicago: Facts and Opinions (*Distinguishing between fact and opinion*) **88**
Dallas: The Main Idea (*Identifying main idea, making inferences, forming questions*) **89**
Using a Pay Telephone (*Following and naming a sequence, using present progressive*) **90**
Dear Dot (*Reading comprehension, making judgments*) **91**

UNIT 9   When and Where

Watch the Clock (*Telling time to the nearest five minutes*) **92**
Time Zones (*Interpreting a map, computing time zone differences*) **93**
Where Are They Going? (*Using present progressive as future, using going to future, making inferences*) **94**
Pronouns (*Using pronouns and possessives*) **95**
Going Places (*Understanding uses of* going, going to, *drawing conclusions*) **96**
A Trip to the Big Apple (*Identifying main idea, making inferences, asking questions*) **97**
A Field Trip (*Identifying main idea and details*) **98**
Dear Dot (*Reading comprehension, making judgments, writing a letter*) **99**

UNIT 10 Chores and Pleasures

What Do You Have to Do? (*Using* have to, has to, *drawing conclusions*) 100

Can and Can't (*Using modals* can, can't, *writing a story*) 101

Interviewing: Can You? (*Using modals* can, can't, *interviewing, using a chart*) 102

A Bike Trip (*Interpreting a diagram, reading for details*) 103

Jack's Car (*Interpreting a diagram, making inferences, writing a paragraph*) 104

Road Signs (*Interpreting road signs*) 105

More Road Signs (*Interpreting road signs, understanding modals* have to, can, can't) 106

Dear Dot (*Reading comprehension, making judgments, writing a letter*) 107

UNIT 11 Health, the Weather, and Social Engagements

Parts of the Body (*Building vocabulary, labeling a diagram, discussing ailments*) 108

A Visit to the Doctor (*Sequencing events, using health-related vocabulary*) 109

How's the Weather? (*Building vocabulary, making inferences*) 110

What and Why? (*Recognizing cause and effect*) 111

The Dinner Party (*Identifying main idea and details, making inferences and judgments*) 112

Crossword Puzzle (*Understanding word definitions, using context clues*) 113

Dear Dot (*Reading comprehension, making judgments, writing a letter*) 114

Vocabulary Review 115–122

End of Book Test

Completing Familiar Structures 123–124
Writing Questions 125
Reading for Details 126

Sample Paragraph (For student reference) 127

Skills Index 128

What's Your Name?

A. Answer the questions. The first two are done for you.

1. What is her first name?

   _____Rita._____

2. What is her last name?

   _____Gonzales._____

3. Where is she from?

   _____

4. What is his first name?

   _____

5. What is his last name?

   _____

6. Where is he from?

   _____

My name is Rita Gonzales. I'm from Mexico.

My name is Dao Nguyen. I'm from Los Angeles.

B. How about you? Answer these questions.

1. What is your first name?

   _____

2. What is your last name?

   _____

3. Where are you from?

   _____

DATA BANK

he	is	last	what
her	first	name	where
his	from	she	

Skill Objective: Introducing oneself and others. Go over Part A orally with the class. Be sure they understand the concept of *first name* and *last name.* Help them to see how they can answer the questions by reading the "speech balloons." Encourage students to introduce themselves using the structures: "My name is . . . I'm from . . ." Check classmates' understanding by asking: "What's her/his first (last) name?" "Where's he/she from?" Introduce yourself using the same structures and follow-up questions. Be sure to write your name on the board. Briefly review the questions in Part B orally, then assign the page for independent written work.

9

Names, Addresses, and Numbers

A. Answer the question.

Easy-Air

NAME - NOMBRE - NOM
Mary Johnson

ADDRESS - DIRECCION - ADRESSE
30 Tower Road

CITY - CIUDAD - VILLE
Sunnyvale

STATE - ESTADO - PROVINCIA - ETAT
California

TELEPHONE - TELEFONO
TELEPHONE
245-5163

ZIP CODE - ZONA POSTAL
- CODE POSTAL
94087

1. What is her first name? _____

2. What is her last name? _____

3. What is her address?

_____

_____

4. What is her zip code? _____

5. What is her telephone number?

_____

B. Answer the questions. The first two are done for you.

1. Is his first name Peter? ___*Yes, it is.*___

2. Is his last name Smith? ___*No, it isn't.*___

3. What is his phone number? _____

4. Is his zip code 02117? _____

Easy-Air

NAME - NOMBRE - NOM
Peter Carlson

ADDRESS - DIRECCION - ADRESSE
22 Hunt St.

CITY - CIUDAD - VILLE
Quincy

STATE - ESTADO - PROVINCIA - ETAT
Mass.

TELEPHONE - TELEFONO
- TELEPHONE
926-3586

ZIP CODE - ZONA POSTAL
- CODE POSTAL
02170

5. Is her last name Linda? _____

6. What is her library card number? _____

7. What is her phone number? _____

8. What is her address? _____

_____

Linda Sutton
38 Whitcome Ave.   Tel.
Chicago, Ill.   949-2901

is entitled to borrow books from the

READING PUBLIC LIBRARY

and is responsible for all use made of this card WHICH
MUST BE PRESENTED each time a book is borrowed.

1381   № 7381

C. How About You? Write the information on *your* card!

IDENTIFICATION

Name _____

Street _____

City _____

State _____ Zip _____

Telephone _____

Skill Objective: Discussing address labels, library cards, ID cards. Teach or review the vocabulary used on these forms. *Part A:* Practice reading the first label with the class. *Part B:* Have a student read the Peter Carlson label aloud. Ask: "What state does Peter live in?" Discuss how state names are abbreviated. Have students answer the questions orally. *Part C:* Let volunteers dictate their addresses and phone numbers to the rest of the class. Write each address and phone number on the board so the students can correct their writing. Then assign the page for independent work.

Classroom Language

1. Please _____ down.

2. _____ at this.

3. _____ your hand.

4. _____ your books.

5. _____ to this.

6. _____ with a _____ .

7. _____ your books.

8. _____ on the _____ .

D A T A B A N K

Look at this.
Open your books.
Please sit down.
Raise your hand.

Work with a partner.
Close your books.
Write on the board.
Listen to this.

Skill Objective: Understanding classroom commands. Introduce each command by reading the sentence and pointing to the picture. Then have the students act out the correct response as you repeat the commands several times, first in sequence and then in random order. Keep the pace lively during this activity. If appropriate, have students give commands to each other. As the final activity, assign this page for independent written work. If necessary, students may refer to the Data Bank as they fill in the missing words.

Things to Remember

1. _____*Walk*_____ in the hall.

2. Don't _____ in the hall.

3. Be on _____ for class.

4. Don't come _____.

5. _____ your hand.

6. Don't _____ out in class.

7. Pay _____ to your teacher.

8. Don't _____ in class.

9. Do your _____.

10. Don't chew _____.

D A T A   B A N K

Be on time for class.
Pay attention to your teacher.
Walk in the hall.
Do your homework.

Raise your hand.
Don't whisper in class.
Don't run in the hall.

Don't chew gum.
Don't come late.
Don't shout out in class.

Skill Objective: Understanding school rules. Review these school rules with the class, reading each directive aloud and studying the pictures together. Act out one of the misdemeanors (example: coming late to class). Let the class give the rule that points out what you have done wrong ("Don't come late") and the rule that tells what you should do ("Be on time"). Let volunteers act out the other misdemeanors; have the class correct them by giving the appropriate rule(s). Then assign the page for independent written work.

Which Way?

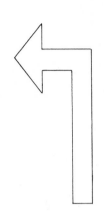 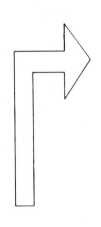  

1. _____left_____

2. _____

3. _____

4. _____

5. _____

6. _____

7. _____

8. _____

DATA BANK

down	left	on	right
in	off	out	up

Skill Objective: Understanding direction words. Teach and practice *left/right* by giving students "marching" directions: "Turn left. Walk 1, 2, 3. Turn right." etc. To practice *up/down*, tell the class: "Point up. Point down. Point right." Steadily increase the speed of these directions. Help the class name the picture pairs on this page, then ask for names in random order, "Number 7. What is it?" Have the class read the prepositions in the Data Bank and find the matching pictures. Assign the page for independent written work.

At School

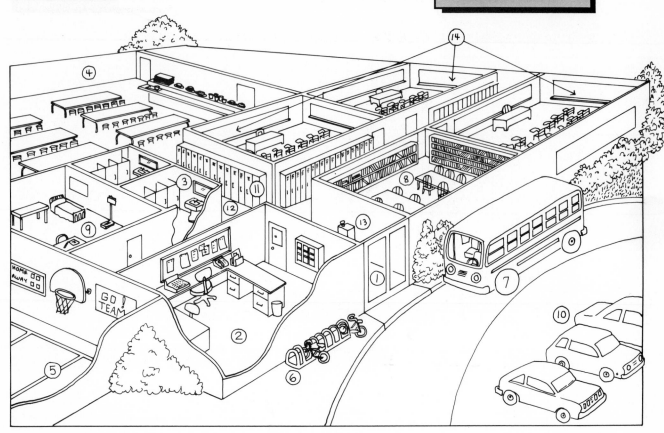

Find the number in the picture. Write the word on the line.

1. _____ *entrance* _____   8. _____

2. _____   9. _____

3. _____   10. _____

4. _____   11. _____

5. _____   12. _____

6. _____   13. _____

7. _____   14. _____

D A T A   B A N K

bathroom	bike rack	classrooms	hallway
library	lockers	cafeteria	nurse's office
office	parking lot	gym	school bus
water fountain			entrance

Skill Objectives: Naming school locations; reading a map. Help students identify the fourteen locations numbered on the school map. Provide practice with the terms by asking: "Where is the (office)? *(It's number 2.)* Do we have an (office) in our school? What is number . . .? Where do we (eat lunch, leave our bikes)?" Adjust the time spent on this oral activity to the needs and skill level of your students. Assign the page for independent written work. Students may refer to the Data Bank as needed.

14

People and Places at School

A. Who is she? Who is he? Write the words. The first one is done for you.

1. _principal_

2. _____

3. _____

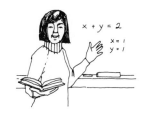

4. _____

5. _____

6. _____

D A T A   B A N K

| bus driver | gym teacher | librarian | math teacher | nurse | principal |

B. Where is he? Where is she? Write the words. The first one is done for you.

1. _gym_

2. _____

3. _____

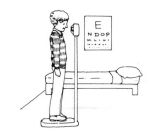

4. _____

5. _____

6. _____

D A T A   B A N K

| classroom | library | nurse's office | hallway | cafeteria | gym |

Skill Objective: Naming school personnel and school locations. Teach or review the vocabulary highlighted on the page. Relate the terms to your school by asking: "Who is the (principal) in our school? Who is your (math teacher)? Where is the (water fountain)?" Go over both parts of the page orally, adjusting the amount of oral practice to the needs of your students. Then assign the page for independent written work.

Number Names

0	1	2	3	4	5	6	7	8	9	10
zero	one	two	three	four	five	six	seven	eight	nine	ten

11	12	13	14	15	16	17
eleven	twelve	thirteen	fourteen	fifteen	sixteen	seventeen

18	19	20	21	30	40	50	60
eighteen	nineteen	twenty	twenty-one	thirty	forty	fifty	sixty

70	80	90	100	101	1000
seventy	eighty	ninety	one hundred	one hundred one	one thousand

A. Write the number names.

1 _____one_____

19 _____

5 _____

300 _____

20 _____

90 _____

3 _____

17 _____

201 _____

220 _____

88 _____

308 _____

6000 _____

70 _____

33 _____

B. Write the numbers.

twenty-seven _____27_____

forty-three _____

nine _____

one hundred five _____

C. Write the number names in the boxes.

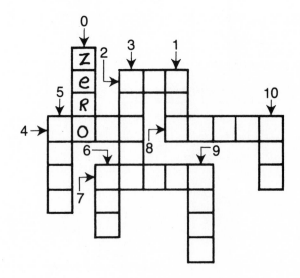

Skill Objective: Naming numbers 1 - 10,000. Use any or all of the following introductory activities, depending on the needs of the students. 1. Have students count from 1 to 100, either in chorus or in sequence, going around the room. If possible, display a number chart. 2. Write random numbers on the board for volunteers to name. 3. Name a number from 1 to 10,000, and have students write the numeral at their desks. Write the answer on the board so that students can immediately check and correct their work. Then review the directions and assign the page for independent written work.

What Time Is It?

Write the sentence. The first one is done for you.

1:00

It's one o'clock.

1 _____

2:00

2 _____

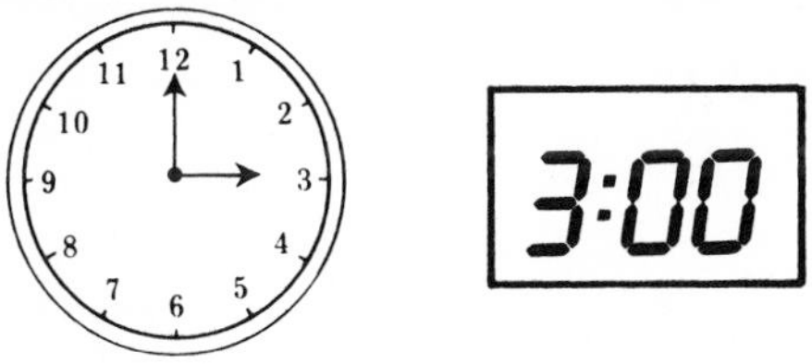

3:00

3 _____

4:00

4 _____

5:00

5 _____

6:00

6 _____

7:00

7 _____

8:00

8 _____

9:00

9 _____

10:00

10 _____

11:00

11 _____

12:00

12 _____

Skill Objective: Telling time on the hour. Go over the page as an oral group activity. First, have students read the twelve clocks in sequence. Then ask, "What time is it?" and name the clocks in random order. After sufficient oral practice, assign the page for independent written work.

Matching Times

Write the letter of the matching clock.

___c___ 1. It's six o'clock.

_____ 2. It's twelve o'clock.

_____ 3. It's three o'clock.

_____ 4. It's seven o'clock.

_____ 5. It's four o'clock.

_____ 6. It's nine o'clock.

_____ 7. It's five o'clock.

_____ 8. It's ten o'clock.

_____ 9. It's one o'clock.

_____ 10. It's two o'clock.

_____ 11. It's eleven o'clock.

_____ 12. It's eight o'clock.

a.   `3:00`

b. `9:00`

c. `6:00`

d. `5:00`

e. `7:00`

f. `12:00`

g. `10:00`

h. `1:00`

i.   `4:00`

j.   `11:00`

k.   `2:00`

l. `8:00`

Skill Objective: Telling time on the hour. Draw attention to the clocks on the right side of the page. Name a clock by its letter, and ask a student to tell the time. Give all students a chance to respond at least once to the question, "What time is it?" For further practice, state a time ("It's ten o'clock.") and have students identify, by letter, the correct clock. After sufficient practice, assign this page for independent work.

Where Is It?

Use a picture to help you learn new words and describe location.

Where's the window?   It's on the left.

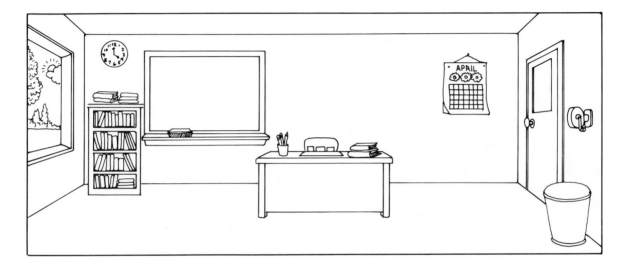

Learn the names of the things in the picture. Then answer the questions. The first one is done for you.

1. Where's the bookcase? ___*It's on the left.*_____

2. Where's the door? _____

3. Where's the board? _____

4. Where's the clock? _____

5. Where's the calendar? _____

6. Where's the pencil sharpener? _____

7. Where's the eraser? _____

8. Where's the waste paper basket? _____

🄳🄰🄳🄰 🄱🄰🄽🄺

on the left   on the right

Skill Objectives: Naming classroom furniture and objects; distinguishing left and right. Review the concept of left and right. Ask, "Raise your right hand, your left hand. Point to the right, to the left," etc. Go over the vocabulary in the picture and have students point to the same items in your classroom. Ask about these items in your room, "Where's the (window)?" and elicit the response, "It's on the (right)." Go through the eight questions orally with the class, then assign the page for independent written work.

Tell When, Tell Where

Sunday

Monday

Tuesday

Wednesday

Thursday

Friday

Saturday

The Days of the Week

Sunday	Monday	Tuesday	Wednesday	Thursday	Friday	Saturday
SUN	MON	TUES	WED	THURS	FRI	SAT
S	M	T	W	T or TH	F	S

WHEN

Look at the pictures. Then answer the questions. The first one is done for you.

1. When is Mike at the park? _____ *On Sunday.* _____

2. When is Mike in the hallway? _____

3. When is Mike at the movies? _____

4. When is Mike at the water fountain? _____

5. When is Mike in the cafeteria? _____

6. When is Mike at the nurse's office? _____

7. When is Mike in the library? _____

WHERE

Look at the pictures again. Then answer the questions. The first one is done for you.

1. Where is Mike on Monday? _____ *In the library.* _____

2. Where is Mike on Wednesday? _____

3. Where is Mike on Saturday? _____

4. Where is Mike on Friday? _____

5. Where is Mike on Tuesday? _____

6. Where is Mike on Thursday? _____

7. Where is Mike on Sunday? _____

Skill Objectives: Naming the days of the week; using pictures to answer questions. Teach or review the days of the week. If possible let students examine several calendars and note the different abbreviations used. Point out that in the United States, Sunday is considered the first day of the week. (In many countries, calendars show the week starting with Monday.) Do several examples from both the "When" part and the "Where" part orally with the class, showing how the pictures are used to provide the answers. Then assign the page for independent written work.

The Months of the Year

Use a calendar to help you learn to say dates.

JANUARY	FEBRUARY	MARCH
S M T W T F S	**S M T W T F S**	**S M T W T F S**
1 2 3 4 5 6 7	1 2 3 4	1 2 3
8 9 10 11 12 13 14	5 6 7 8 9 10 11	4 5 6 7 8 9 10
15 16 17 18 19 20 21	12 13 14 15 16 17 18	11 12 13 14 15 16 17
22 23 24 25 26 27 28	19 20 21 22 23 24 25	18 19 20 21 22 23 24
29 30 31	26 27 28 29	25 26 27 28 29 30 31

APRIL	MAY	JUNE
S M T W T F S	**S M T W T F S**	**S M T W T F S**
1 2 3 4 5 6 7	1 2 3 4 5	1 2
8 9 10 11 12 13 14	6 7 8 9 10 11 12	3 4 5 6 7 8 9
15 16 17 18 19 20 21	13 14 15 16 17 18 19	10 11 12 13 14 15 16
22 23 24 25 26 27 28	20 21 22 23 24 25 26	17 18 19 20 21 22 23
29 30	27 28 29 30 31	24 25 26 27 28 29 30

JULY	AUGUST	SEPTEMBER
S M T W T F S	**S M T W T F S**	**S M T W T F S**
1 2 3 4 5 6 7	1 2 3 4	1
8 9 10 11 12 13 14	5 6 7 8 9 10 11	2 3 4 5 6 7 8
15 16 17 18 19 20 21	12 13 14 15 16 17 18	9 10 11 12 13 14 15
22 23 24 25 26 27 28	19 20 21 22 23 24 25	16 17 18 19 20 21 22
29 30 31	26 27 28 29 30 31	23 24 25 26 27 28 29 / 30

OCTOBER	NOVEMBER	DECEMBER
S M T W T F S	**S M T W T F S**	**S M T W T F S**
1 2 3 4 5 6	1 2 3	1
7 8 9 10 11 12 13	4 5 6 7 8 9 10	2 3 4 5 6 7 8
14 15 16 17 18 19 20	11 12 13 14 15 16 17	9 10 11 12 13 14 15
21 22 23 24 25 26 27	18 19 20 21 22 23 24	16 17 18 19 20 21 22
28 29 30 31	25 26 27 28 29 30	23 24 25 26 27 28 29 / 30 31

A. Complete each sentence with the correct month. The first one is done for you.

1. May is before _____ *June* _____ .

2. December is after _____ .

3. March is before _____ .

4. August is after _____ .

5. October is after _____ .

6. January is before _____ .

> ### Learn to Say Dates
>
> We write: December 20.
> We say: "December twentieth."
>
> We write: 1992
> We say: "nineteen ninety-two."
>
> Your teacher can help you to say other dates.

B. We can write dates two ways: 6/9/90 and June 9, 1990.

The month always comes first. "6" stands for June because June is the sixth month.

On your paper, write each date *the other way.*

1. April 4, 1991
2. 7/1/90
3. January 24, 1990
4. 2/9/91
5. May 17, 1993
6. 10/12/92
7. November 8, 1992
8. 3/13/94
9. 8/30/90
10. September 14, 1995
11. 12/25/93
12. June 2, 1991

Skill Objectives: Reading a calendar; naming the months; understanding *before* and *after*. *Part A:* Teach/review the names of the months. Give 12 students cards with the name of a month on each card; have them read their cards and line up in order (January, February, March, etc.). Repeat with other students. Teach or review "before" and "after." Ask, "What month is before (June)? What month is after (March)? Is July after August?" etc. *Part B:* On the board, explain the two ways of writing dates given on the page. Do the first three or four items orally before assigning the page for independent work.

Reading a Calendar

SEPTEMBER

S	M	T	W	TH	F	S
		1	2	3	4	5 Family Party
6	7	8	First day of class 9	10	11	12
13	14	15	16	17	18	19
20	Don's birthday 21	22	soccer game 23	24	25	Sue's birthday 26
27	28	Doctor's Appointment 29	30			

A. Look at the calendar and the Data Bank. Answer the questions using words from the Data Bank. The first one is done for you.

1. When is the first day of class?   *It's September ninth.*

2. When is the family party?   _____

3. When is the soccer game?   _____

4. When is Don's birthday?   _____

5. When is Sue's birthday?   _____

6. When is the doctor's appointment?   _____

DATA BANK

1 first	11 eleventh	21 twenty-first
2 second	12 twelfth	22 twenty-second
3 third	13 thirteenth	23 twenty-third
4 fourth	14 fourteenth	24 twenty-fourth
5 fifth	15 fifteenth	25 twenty-fifth
6 sixth	16 sixteenth	26 twenty-sixth
7 seventh	17 seventeenth	27 twenty-seventh
8 eighth	18 eighteenth	28 twenty-eighth
9 ninth	19 nineteenth	29 twenty-ninth
10 tenth	20 twentieth	30 thirtieth

B. Fill in more boxes on the calendar. Show your calendar to a friend and ask and answer questions like the ones above.

Skill Objectives: Reading a calendar; reporting dates. Ask students, "What's the date today? What day of the week is it?" Review the days of the week; call attention to the way they are abbreviated on this calendar. Introduce ordinal numbers by counting the days on the calendar together out loud: "first, second, . . ." *Part A:* Do several of the questions orally before assigning them for independent work. *Part B:* Work with students orally to fill three or four boxes on the calendar. Have them fill in others. Then divide the class into pairs to ask and answer questions about their calendars.

22

May I?

A. Read these dialogues with a friend.

May I go to the bathroom, please?

Yes, you may.

nurse   office   library

May I open the window, please?

No, You may not.

sharpen my pencil   erase the board   call home

B. Write the questions.

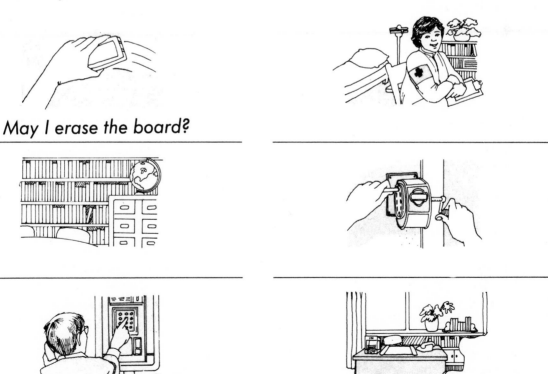

May I erase the board?

_____   _____

_____   _____

_____   _____

Skill Objective: Asking permission. Teach or review the vocabulary on the page. Let students ask one another permission to go places and do things. They should use the forms "May I . . ., please?" and "Yes, you may./No, you may not." Students need not restrict themselves to the places and actions pictured. Be sure all students have a chance to participate in this oral practice. Assign the page for independent written work.

Talking About Feelings

A. Look at the pictures. Talk about each word.

I feel homesick.

confused

tired   angry   sad   sick   nervous

B. Write a dialogue for each picture. The first two are done for you. Use them as examples.

1. A: *What's the matter?*
   B: *I feel confused.*
   A: *Maybe I can help.*
   B: *Thanks.*

2. A: *How do you feel?*
   B: *Not so good.*
   A: *What's wrong?*
   B: *I feel angry.*

3. _____
   _____
   _____
   _____

4. _____
   _____
   _____
   _____

5. _____
   _____
   _____
   _____

6. _____
   _____
   _____
   _____

C. Now practice your dialogues with a friend or classmate.

Skill Objectives: Describing feelings; writing short dialogues. Teach or review the vocabulary highlighted on this page. *Part A:* Have the class mime the emotions illustrated at the top of the page. Each time ask, "What's the matter?" or "How do you feel?" The class will respond, "I/We feel . . ." Then encourage students to ask one another these questions and respond as they choose. *Part B:* On the board, do items 1 and 2 together so that students understand how to write the dialogue. Discuss other possible responses (for example, "That's too bad," "I'm sorry" for item 1). Then assign the page for independent written work.

Class Rules

GOOD MORNING !

THIS IS MRS. CHACON'S ENGLISH I CLASS AT ALLSTON HIGH SCHOOL.

TODAY IS WEDNESDAY , SEPT. 9

CLASS RULES

1. BE ON TIME FOR CLASS.
2. RAISE YOUR HAND TO ANSWER A QUESTION.
3. PAY ATTENTION TO YOUR TEACHER.
4. LISTEN.
5. DO YOUR HOMEWORK.

Answer the following questions. Fill in the circle. The first one is done for you.

1. What day is it?
   a. Monday
   b. Tuesday
   c. Wednesday ⓐ ⓑ ●

2. What is the date?
   a. Sept. 3
   b. Sept. 9
   c. Sept. 4 ⓐ ⓑ ⓒ

3. What is the name of the high school?
   a. Arlington High School
   b. Austin High School
   c. Allston High School ⓐ ⓑ ⓒ

4. Who is the teacher?
   a. Mrs. Johnson
   b. Mr. Allston
   c. Mrs. Chacon ⓐ ⓑ ⓒ

5. What is NOT a rule in Mrs. Chacon's class?
   a. Raise your hand to answer a question.
   b. Pay attention to the teacher.
   c. Shout out in class. ⓐ ⓑ ⓒ

6. What is the name of the class?
   a. English 1
   b. Allston
   c. French ⓐ ⓑ ⓒ

Skill Objective: Reading rules and information. Review vocabulary from pages 11 and 12 if necessary. Call on volunteers to read the message on the "chalkboard" at the top of the page. Ask students questions about the message, for example, "What day is it? What's the date?" Do questions 1 and 2 together. Emphasize that students are to choose only one answer for each question. Show them how to "fill in the circle" to indicate their answer. Then assign the page for independent work. NOTE: This format is used here and elsewhere to give students practice in one kind of standardized test question setup.

25

Clothing

Use pictures to help you learn the names of clothing.

1.
2.
3.
4.
5.
6.

7.
8.
9.
10.
11.
12.

13.
14.
15.
16.
17.
18.

Find the picture. Write the sentence. The first one is done for you.

1. _____ *It's a hat.* _____
2. _____
3. _____
4. _____
5. _____
6. _____
7. _____
8. _____
9. _____

10. _____
11. _____
12. _____
13. _____
14. _____
15. _____
16. _____
17. _____
18. _____

D A T A   B A N K

pair of shorts	shirt	pair of socks	scarf	hat
tie	raincoat	pair of glasses	jacket	dress
pair of jeans	belt	pair of boots	sweater	skirt
blouse	bathrobe	pair of sneakers		

Skill Objective: Naming articles of clothing. Teach or review the clothing vocabulary highlighted on this page. Call attention to the Data Bank and point out in particular the items referred to as "a pair of . . ." Have students quiz each other on the clothing vocabulary in a chain conversation: Student A, "What's number (six)?" Student B, "It's a (raincoat)." (To Student C): "What's number (eleven)?" etc. After sufficient oral practice, assign the page as independent written work.

What Are They Wearing?

Write what each person is wearing. The first one is done for you.

1. *She is wearing a T-shirt and a pair of shorts.*

2. _____

3. _____

4. _____

5. _____

6. _____

7. _____

8. _____

Skill Objectives: Discussing clothes; writing descriptions. Review clothing vocabulary by making a statement about what you are wearing. ("I am wearing a blouse, a skirt, and a sweater.") Ask students, "What are you wearing?" "What is (Maria) wearing?" Have students read the description written next to the first picture. In each description, students should list two items the person is wearing. Have the class do all or some of the page orally before you assign it as written work. Listen for correct use of the pronouns *he* and *she*.

Counting American Money

Use pictures to help you count money.

A. How much is it worth? Write the words. The first one is done for you.

a penny	a nickel	a dime	a quarter	a half dollar

one cent _____ _____ _____ _____

25¢ .25	50¢ .50	10¢ .10	1¢ .01	5¢ .05
twenty-five cents	fifty cents	ten cents	one cent	five cents
quarter	half dollar	dime	penny	nickel

B. How much money do you have? Write the numbers. The first one is done for you.

1.  $1.45

2.    _____

3.    _____

C. Write the amount. The first one is done for you.

1. $2.63   *two dollars and sixty-three cents*

2. $5.05   _____

3. $7.99   _____

4. $20.22   _____

5. $4.36   _____

Skill Objectives: Counting money; reading and writing prices. Bring coins and bills to class. Have students practice counting money, reporting and writing each amount as a number and a phrase. *Part A:* Have the class identify the value of each coin, then let students write the answers. *Part B:* Teach the two notations for amounts under a dollar: .39 and 39¢. Assign Part B, then correct and discuss as a class. *Part C:* Have students read the prices aloud. Note that $2.63 is read as "two sixty-three," but written as *two dollars and sixty-three cents*.

Money Problems

Use what you already know to answer questions about money.

Answer these questions.

1. Ben has a penny, two dimes, three nickels, and a quarter. *How much* money is this?

   _____

2. Mary is buying a scarf. It is eight dollars and fifty cents. She has a ten dollar bill. How much is Mary's *change*?

   _____

3. A shoe store is having a sale. Mrs. Yakos is buying two pairs of sneakers. How much money is that?

   _____

4. Look at the sweater, the pair of jeans, and the pair of boots. Willie has a twenty dollar bill.

   Can he buy the sweater, jeans, and boots? _____

   Can he buy the sweater and the jeans? _____

   Can he buy the sweater? _____

   How much is his change? _____

5. This is the Baxter family. They are eating chicken dinners. *Each* dinner is $5.00. How much is the bill?

   _____

6. James and June are *twins.* It's their birthday today. Their father and mother are giving them $30.00. The twins are *dividing* the money *evenly.* How much is June's present?

   _____

Categories

A. Circle the word that doesn't belong. The first one is done for you.

1. Bob, Paul, (Mary,) Dick

2. five, seven, first, ten

3. street, avenue, road, skirt

4. Monday, Thursday, Friday, March

5. red, yes, blue, yellow

6. blouse, shoes, boots, sandals

7. teacher, library, principal, nurse

8. wearing, looking, sitting, morning

9. she, they, his, I

10. brown, blouse, blue, pink

B. Add one word which belongs in the category. The first one is done for you.

1. slippers, sneakers, boots, _sandals_____

2. tennis, baseball, football, _____

3. slacks, trousers, jeans, _____

4. she, he, it, _____

5. February, October, July, _____

6. New York, Texas, California, _____

7. sister, father, mother, _____

8. zip code, street, name, _____

C. Remembering: **Study the picture below as long as you wish. When you think you can remember the names of all or most of the items, close the book. On another piece of paper write the names of the items you remember. There are eight items. Then compare your list with the picture.**

Skill Objectives: Classifying; memorizing. *Part A:* Discuss the first example as a class, then have students do the remaining items. You may wish to let students work in pairs on this section and then discuss and correct it as a class. *Part B:* Do the first three items orally as a class to be sure students understand what to do. Again, students may work in pairs. *Part C:* Be sure students know the names of clothing items before they try memorizing them. This could be a contest between two or more students to see who can remember the most.

Missing Words

A. Write in a word to complete the sentence. The first one is done for you.

1. Tom is ___*wearing*___ a green jacket.

2. What _____ is his shirt?

3. Is _____ your hat?

4. Mary isn't wearing a _____ dress.

5. Fred and Paul _____ friends.

6. This is _____ friend.

7. _____ is wearing a yellow sweater?

8. Is _____ name Peter?

B. Fill in the missing words.

1. —Is this your umbrella?

   —No, ___*that*___ is my umbrella.

2. —Who _____ wearing blue jeans?

   —Bob _____.

3. —What's _____?

   —It's a bathrobe.

4. —What is Sally _____?

   —She's _____ a white blouse.

5. —Is _____ coat black?

   —No, _____ is blue.

6. —Is _____ friend wearing a coat?

   —No, _____ isn't.

Skill Objectives: Recognizing and completing familiar phrases; using context clues. On this page, students use context clues to complete simple sentences and dialogues. Do several examples as a class. Draw attention to the fact that a number of different responses can be correct: "What *color* is his shirt?"/"What *size* is his shirt?" "Is *this* your hat?"/"Is *that* your hat?" Have students complete the page independently. Then discuss their answers as a class.

The Four Seasons

Many parts of the United States have four very different seasons. Winter is the cold season from December to March. Spring is a warm and rainy season. It lasts from March until June. Summer is the hot time of the year from June until September. The autumn or fall is a cool time of year. It is from September until December.

   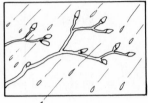

_____   _____   _____   _____

A. **Look at the pictures. Each shows one season. Write the name of the season under each picture.**

B. **Read each description and answer the question after it.**

1. Frannie is wearing a hat, her gloves, a big coat, and boots.

   What season is it? _____

2. Jack is outside. He is wearing shorts and a T-shirt. He's not wearing shoes.

   What season is it? _____

3. Maria is going to a party. She puts on a light jacket and takes her umbrella.

   What season is it? _____

4. Raul is wearing a shirt and sweater and long pants. He is going to a football game.

   What season is it? _____

C. **Tell what season each month is in.**

1. January _____   5. February _____

2. July _____   6. November _____

3. October _____   7. August _____

4. May _____   8. April _____

D A T A   B A N K

coat	football	gloves	spring	umbrella
fall	game	pants	summer	winter

Skill Objectives: Reading for details; making inferences. Discuss seasons with the class. Ask, "What season is it now?" Establish that in many northern hemisphere countries there are four distinct seasons. Then read the story aloud. Point out that it refers to "many parts of the United States." (In southern hemisphere countries the seasons are reversed.) *Part A:* Do the first picture with the class. Ask why they think the picture shows fall. Let them do the other pictures. *Part B:* Do the first question orally. Let them complete the others independently. *Part C:* Do several questions with the class, then let them complete the others independently.

Asking Questions

> **Question Words**
>
> "Who" asks about a person: John, my friends, the girls.
> "What" asks about a thing: the desk, my books, the houses.
> "Where" asks about a place: at school, in the house.
> "When" asks about a time: at 3:00, in January, on Monday.

A. Match the questions to the answers. Write the letter on the line. The first one is done for you.

1. Who is your teacher? ___d___   a. It's at 9:00.

2. Where is Mike? _____   b. He's my friend, Jose.

3. What is Paul wearing? _____   c. It's in France.

4. When is the party? _____   d. Mrs. Chacon is my teacher.

5. Who is that boy? _____   e. It's in December.

6. Where is Paris? _____   f. He's wearing a blue sweater.

7. When is Christmas? _____   g. She's wearing a red dress.

8. What is Mary wearing? _____   h. He's in the cafeteria.

B. Now you try. Look at the Data Bank below. Find a question for each answer. The first one is done for you.

1. ___Where is Susan_____ ? She's at the nurse's office.

2. _____ ? Mr. Tyson is my teacher.

3. _____ ? It's in September.

4. _____ ? She's wearing a green dress.

5. _____ ? It's at 10:00.

6. _____ ? It's in the United States.

DATA BANK

Where is Susan?	**When is your English class?**
Where is New York?	**What is Susan wearing?**
Who is your teacher?	**When is Labor Day?**

Skill Objective: Asking and writing wh- questions. Discuss the Question Words in the box and give an example of a question or two using each one. *Part A:* Do the first two matching questions together to be sure that students understand that they are to write the letter of the matching answer next to each question. *Part B:* Call attention to the Data Bank. Work through the items orally before assigning the page for independent or pair work.

Flags, Countries, and Continents

Every country has its own flag. The flag uses the special colors of the country.

Many flags are red, white, and blue. The flags of the United States, France, Puerto Rico, and the Dominican Republic are all red, white, and blue. So are many others.

The flag of Portugal is red and green. Colombia's flag is yellow, blue, and red. The flag of Japan is white with a red ball in the middle of it. The Soviet Union's flag is red with a yellow design on it.

Many flags have stars and stripes on them. The United States' flag has more stars than any other country's. It has 50 stars. Each star stands for one state in the United States. Some people call the United States' flag "The Stars and Stripes."

A. Read the story and answer the following questions on a separate sheet of paper.

1. How are the flags of the United States, France, Puerto Rico, and the Dominican Republic the same?

2. What colors are in the flag of Portugal?

3. What country's flag is white with a red ball in the middle?

4. What color is the flag of the Soviet Union?

5. How is the United States' flag different from all others?

6. What do some people call the United States flag?

B. On your own paper, make a chart like this one. Use the names of the countries in the box to complete your chart. Use an atlas or an encyclopedia if you need to.

Continents				
Asia	Africa	North America	South America	Europe
China	Egypt			

Countries

Argentina	Chile	Greece	Norway	Venezuela
Brazil	China	Japan	Senegal	Vietnam
Cambodia	Egypt	Lebanon	Switzerland	Zaire
Canada	France	Mexico	United States	Zimbabwe

C. Name other countries that are on each of the five continents above. Use an atlas or an encyclopedia if you need to.

Skill Objectives: Reading to find facts; making a chart to organize information. Review color names if necessary. If you have an American flag in the room, have students name its colors. If possible, show pictures of other flags and ask students to describe them. Read the story aloud. *Part A:* Work through several items as a class. Then have students complete the Part. *Part B:* Show the continents on a world map, have students find Asia and China, Africa and Egypt. Then have students make and complete their charts. *Part C:* Have volunteers suggest other countries in each continent. Then have the class add these and others to their charts.

What's the Time?

A. Write the sentence. The first two are done for you.

1. _It's three o'clock._ 2. _It's quarter to six._ 3. _____ 4. _____

5. _____ 6. _____ 7. _____ 8. _____

9. _____ 10. _____ 11. _____ 12. _____

B. Look at the signs and answer the questions. The first two are done for you.

LACY'S SHOES	**U.S. POST OFFICE**	**FIRST BANK**
Hours	*Hours*	*Hours*
Monday–Saturday	Monday to Friday	Monday–Friday
9:30 AM to 9:30 PM	8:00–6:00	8:30–3:30
Sunday: 12:00–6:00	Saturday: 8:00–12:00	Saturday: 9–12

1. What are Lacy's hours on Tuesday? _9:30 AM – 9:30 PM._____

2. Is Lacy's open on Sunday? _Yes, it is._____

3. What are the hours at the Post Office on Monday? _____

4. When is the Post Office open on Saturday? _____

5. What are the bank's hours on Thursday? _____

6. Is the bank open on Saturday? _____

Skill Objectives: Telling time; reading signs. Review telling time on the hour. If possible use a practice clock with movable hands to teach (or review) "quarter to . . .," "quarter past . . .," and "half past . . ." *Part A:* Work through part or all of the items in an oral group exercise before assigning them for written work. *Part B:* Read the signs aloud. Have students read "12:00-6:00" as "from twelve to six." Discuss the need for this kind of information. Have pairs of students ask each other the six questions and make up questions of their own. Then assign the page for independent written work.

Barrington Bus Company

★ *Daily Service* ★

Tickets:

One way—$8.00
Round trip—$15.00

Barrington to Plymouth

Leaves Barrington	Arrives Plymouth
6:30 a.m.	8:30 a.m.
11:30 a.m.	1:30 p.m.
4:30 p.m.	**6:30 p.m.**

Plymouth to Barrington

Leaves Plymouth	Arrives Barrington
9:00 a.m.	11:00 a.m.
2:00 p.m.	**4:00 p.m.**
7:00 p.m.	**9:00 p.m.**

Look at the bus schedule. Then write the answer in the blank space. The first one is done for you.

1. The first bus leaves Barrington at ___*6:30 a.m.*___ and arrives in Plymouth at

   _____ .

2. The bus trip from Barrington to Plymouth is _____ hours.

3. The 11:30 a.m. bus arrives in Plymouth at _____ .

4. There are _____ morning trips to Plymouth.

5. A one-way ticket from Barrington to Plymouth is $ _____ .

6. The last bus leaves Barrington at _____ .

7. The first bus leaves Plymouth at _____ and arrives in Barrington at

   _____ .

8. There are _____ bus trips from Plymouth to Barrington every day.

9. A round-trip ticket (from Barrington to Barrington) is $ _____ .

10. You arrive in Plymouth at 8:30 a.m. and spend all day there with a friend. The last bus you

    can take home to Barrington leaves at _____ .

Skill Objective: Reading a bus schedule. Teach/review vocabulary on the bus schedule. Ask questions about bus times and ticket prices. Help students to examine the schedule to find the answers. When they are comfortable with this chart-reading skill, have them look at the sentences below the schedule. Point out that some of the sentences have two blank spaces, some have only one. Demonstrate how to use the schedule to find the answer. Have the class decide on the correct answer for the second blank in item 1. Do Item 2 orally as well, then assign the page for independent work.

In, On, or Under?

Look at the picture and read the sentences next to it.

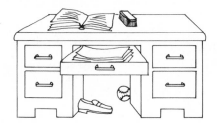

1. The book is *on* the desk.

2. The paper is *in* the desk.

3. The shoe is *under* the desk.

4. The ball is *behind* the desk.

5. The eraser is *next to* the book.

A. Now look at the picture of Anne's Room, and complete the sentences about it by writing *in, on, under, behind,* or *next to.*

1. The socks are _____ the shoes.

2. The jeans are _____ the floor.

3. Anne is _____ the table.

4. The tennis racket is _____ the chair.

5. The boots are _____ the sweater.

6. The blouse is _____ the chair.

7. The bathrobe is _____ the closet.

8. The records are _____ the bed.

Anne's Room

B. On your own paper, write a paragraph about this picture, using the sentences from Part A. Begin your paragraph with the following title and topic sentence.

Anne's Messy Room

Anne's room is messy.

Skill Objectives: Using prepositions *in, on, under, behind, next to*; writing a paragraph. Write the highlighted prepositions on the board and check understanding of their meaning. Call attention to the top picture. Have students read the five sentences and demonstrate where the items are. *Part A:* Have students look at the picture of Anne's room and do the eight questions orally as a class before writing their answers. *Part B:* Discuss the model paragraph on page 127 and tell students they are to write a paragraph about Anne's room using the sentences in Part A. Check for indention, capitalization of first word in a sentence, and period at the end of each sentence.

Where Are My Things?

Write in the answers. The first one is done for you.

1. Where are my shoes?

They're under the bed.

2. Where is my notebook?

3. Where is my green tie?

4. Where are my books?

5. Where are our jackets?

6. Where is my belt?

7. Where are my keys?

Skill Objective: Using prepositions *in, on, under, behind, in front of.* Review the highlighted prepositions, writing them on the board and having students demonstrate each one. *(under, on, in, in front of, behind).* Go through part or all of the page orally before assigning it for independent written work.

The Surprise Party

Today is Mario's birthday. His mother is giving him a surprise party. His new friends Ramon and Thomas are in the living room. They are behind the sofa. Maria is under the table. Antonio is in the closet behind the coats. Carlos, Robert, and Nancy are behind the chairs. Mrs. Mendez is in the kitchen. Mario's brothers and sisters are behind the kitchen door. Everyone is waiting for Mario. They want to yell "Surprise!"

A. Answer the following questions. The first one is done for you.

1. What day is today? _____ *It is Mario's birthday.* _____

2. Where are Ramon and Thomas? _____

_____

3. Who is under the table? _____

4. Where are Carlos, Robert, and Nancy? _____

_____

5. Where are Mario's brothers and sisters? _____

_____

6. What does everyone want to yell? _____

B. What is this story mostly about? Circle the best answer.

a. Mario's new friends

b. Mario's surprise party

c. Mario's happy family

d. Mario's mother

C. Write the name of each person in the place where he or she is hiding. Be sure to include all Mario's friends, his brothers and sisters, and his mother.

Skill Objectives: Identifying main idea and details; following directions. Say, "Today is Mario's birthday. His mother is giving him a surprise party. What do people do at a surprise party? Look at the picture of Mario's house. Where can you hide?" Provide needed vocabulary as students suggest hiding places. Read the story aloud. Answer questions 2 and 3 as a class, then assign Parts A and B as independent work. Discuss Part B when it is done. Remind students to reread the story as they independently complete Part C.

Maps

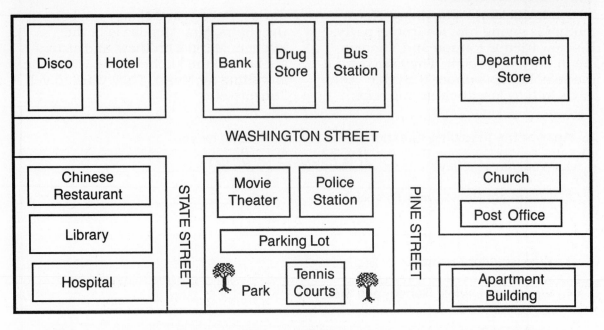

A. **Answer "yes" or "no" to the following statements.** The first one is done for you.

yes 1. The library is *between* the Chinese restaurant and the hospital.

_____ 2. The library is *on* State Street.

_____ 3. The hotel is *next to* the hospital.

_____ 4. The bank is *at the corner of* Washington St. and State St.

_____ 5. The hotel is *across from* the bank.

B. **Use the words at the end of the line to answer these questions.** The first one is done for you.

1. Where is the park? _It's on Broadway._____ (on)

2. Where is the drug store? _____ (between)

3. Where is the church? _____ (at the corner of)

4. Where is the department store? _____ (across from)

5. Where is the post office? _____ (next to)

C. **Answer these questions.** The first one is done for you.

1. Is the parking lot next to the movie theater?   _Yes, it is.___

2. Is the police station between the church and the bank?   _____

3. Is the hospital across from the drug store?   _____

4. Is the bus station at the corner of Pine St. and Washington St.?   _____

5. Are the tennis courts next to the apartment building?   _____

Skill Objectives: Reading a map; using prepositions; giving directions. Ask students, "What streets are on this map? What places are on Washington Street?" (*bank, movie theater, police station,* etc.) "What's at the corner of Washington Street and Pine Street?" (*bus station, police station, church, department store*) On the board write, *on, next to, between, across from.* Ask, "Where's the drugstore?" Point to each preposition to cue a different student answer. *Parts A, B, C:* Go through enough items orally in each section to be sure that students understand what to do before assigning the page for independent work.

Following Directions

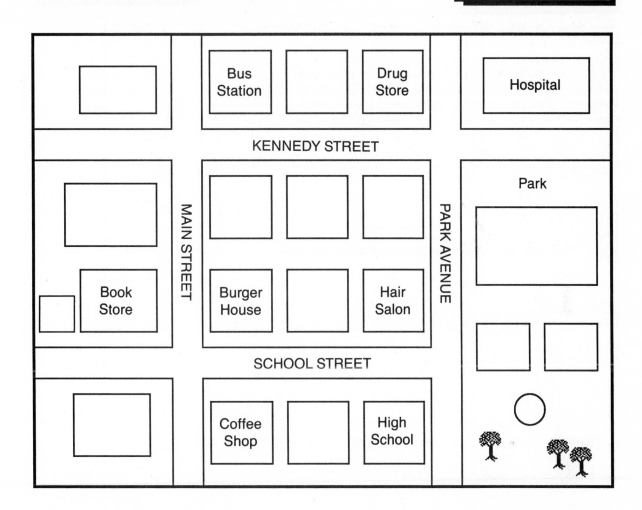

Read the sentences below. Write the name of the place in the correct location on the map.

1. The *hotel* is next to Burger House at the corner of Main St. and Kennedy St.
2. The *bank* is between Burger House and the hair salon on School St.
3. The *parking lot* is aross from the bank, next to the high school.
4. The *gas station* is between the bus station and the drug store on Kennedy St.
5. The *playground* is in the park. The *tennis courts* are in the park too.
6. The *music store* is across the street from the gas station, next to the hotel.
7. The *church* is at the corner of Main St. and School St.
8. The *movie theater* is next to the music store at the corner of Park Ave. and Kennedy St.
9. The *post office* is next to the bookstore at the corner of Main St. and Kennedy St.
10. A *telephone booth* is next to the bookstore.
11. The *library* is at the corner of Main St. and Kennedy St.
12. A *drinking fountain* is near the tennis courts in the park.

Skill Objectives: Reading a map; following directions. On the board write, *on, at the corner of, next to, across from.* Ask volunteers to use these words to describe orally the location of each named place on the map. Go over the instructions for the page and complete the first few items as a class, comparing and correcting each drawing. NOTE: To use this as a listening activity, write the names of the 12 buildings, etc., on the board and have students cover the sentences. Dictate the sentences to the class and have students write the name of each place in the correct location.

The New England States

New England is a group of six states. The six states are Maine, New Hampshire, Vermont, Massachusetts, Rhode Island, and Connecticut.

The states are close together. New Hampshire is between Vermont and Maine. Rhode Island is next to Connecticut. Massachusetts is south of Vermont and New Hampshire. The state of New York is west of New England. The Atlantic Ocean is on the east and south. Canada is north of New England.

A. Answer the following questions. Fill in the circle.

1. Where is New England?
   a. to the east of the Atlantic Ocean
   b. to the south of Canada
   c. to the north of New York

   ⓐ   ⓑ   ⓒ

2. Which is NOT a New England state?
   a. New York
   b. Connecticut
   c. Rhode Island

   ⓐ   ⓑ   ⓒ

3. What state is next to New Hampshire on the east?
   a. Rhode Island
   b. Connecticut
   c. Maine

   ⓐ   ⓑ   ⓒ

4. What country is near New England?
   a. the United States
   b. Canada
   c. England

   ⓐ   ⓑ   ⓒ

B. Look at the map and answer the following questions. Use the words north, south, east, and west.

1. New Hampshire is _____ of Connecticut.

2. New England is _____ of Canada.

3. New England is _____ of New York.

4. Vermont is _____ of New Hampshire.

5. Massachusetts is _____ of Connecticut.

6. Connecticut is _____ of Rhode Island.

C. On your own paper, write about the state or province you live in. Tell what is north, south, east, and west of it.

Skill Objectives: Reading a map; reading to find facts; writing a paragraph. Call attention to the map and pronounce the names of the states and Canada. Then discuss the directions, north, south, east, and west. If you have a map of the United States, you may wish to locate your own state and ask what states are north, south, east, and west of it. Read the story aloud. *Part A:* Do question 1 together to be sure students understand the format. *Part B:* Do sentence 1 orally and make sure students understand why north is the only correct answer. *Part C:* Students may need a U.S. map for this Part. Also, refer them again to the model paragraph on page 127.

Using the Verb "To Be"

| I am (I'm) | She is (She's) | We are (We're) | They are (They're) |
| He is (He's) | It is (It's) | You are (You're) | |

A. Fill in the missing words. The first one is done for you.

Hello. I _____ *am* _____ Binh. I _____ from Vietnam.

This is my class. We _____ from different countries.

She _____ Anna. She _____ from Greece.

He _____ Amin. He _____ from Lebanon.

They _____ Luis and Rosa. They _____ from Mexico.

B. Write the correct form of the verb "to be" in the blank. The first one is done for you.

1. The desk _____ *is* _____ on the left.

2. The students _____ in the gym.

3. We _____ from London, England.

4. You _____ not Chinese.

5. The girls _____ tired.

6. It _____ 3:00.

7. His first name _____ Paul.

8. Mary and Henry _____ nervous about the test.

9. I _____ angry at the boys.

10. My friends _____ from Canada.

11. They _____ homesick for their country, Mexico.

12. September _____ before October.

13. Marjorie _____ wearing a T-shirt today.

14. We _____ all students.

Skill Objective: Reviewing present forms of *to be*. Ask students, "Where are you from? Where is (Paco, Binh) from? Where are (Tomas and Gina) from? Where are you and (Ali) from?" Use the responses to build a chart on the board with all the present forms of "to be" ("I am from . . .," "He is from . . .," etc.). Review the chart together. *Part A:* Do this as an oral exercise before assigning it as independent work. *Part B:* Go over the first two sentences as an oral exercise before assigning the Part as independent work.

43

Anna Garcia

A. Circle the best word. The first one is done for you.

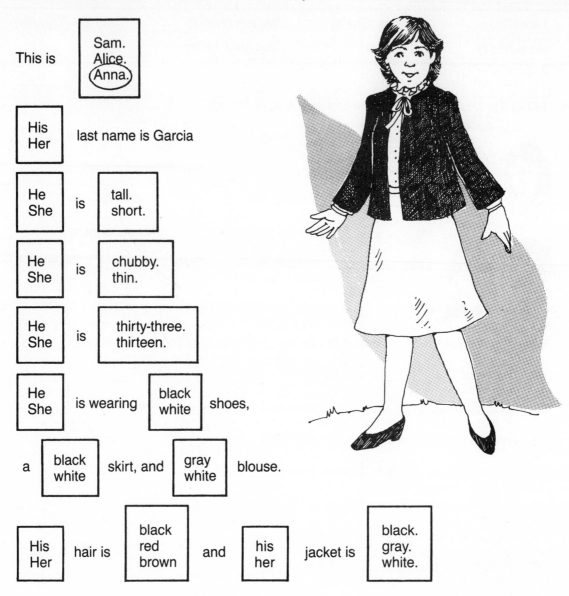

This is | Sam. Alice. (Anna.)

His / Her   last name is Garcia

He / She   is   tall. / short.

He / She   is   chubby. / thin.

He / She   is   thirty-three. / thirteen.

He / She   is wearing   black / white   shoes,

a   black / white   skirt, and   gray / white   blouse.

His / Her   hair is   black red brown   and   his / her   jacket is   black. gray. white.

B. Describe your friend or your favorite star.

_____

_____

_____

_____

_____

Skill Objectives: Reviewing pronouns and adjectives; writing a description. Briefly review the pronouns *he, she, his, her* by asking students questions about their classmates: "What is (Anna's/Mario's) last name?" "Is (Laura/Carlos) tall or short?" "How old is your (sister/brother)?" "What color is (Manuel's) hair?" Do Part A as an oral group exercise before assigning it as independent written work. Explain that students can use Part A as a model as they write their own descriptive paragraph in Part B. (You may wish again to refer students to the model paragraph on page 127 for important parts of paragraph format.)

Describing People and Things

Write the sentences. Use the adjectives in the Data Bank. The first two are done for you.

TED   JAN

1.

84   14

a. _Ted is old._

b. _Jan is young._

2.

LINDA   GINA

a. _____

b. _____

3.

JOSE   CARLOS

a. _____

b. _____

4.

SOFIA   AGATHA

a. _____

b. _____

5.

a. _____

b. _____

6.

THEY   HE

a. _____

b. _____

D A T A   B A N K

thin	young	single	cheap	tall	beautiful
expensive	short	old	married	fat	ugly

Skill Objective: Reviewing adjectives and present forms of *to be*. Encourage students to call out the opposites as you say the following words: *big, fat, expensive, tall, beautiful, old, good, different, sad.* Ask volunteers to orally provide contrasting ("opposite") sentences to go with each pair of sketches on the page. Students can refer to the Data Bank for appropriate adjectives. Assign the page for independent work.

Information, Please

Review

| I am (I'm) | you are (you're) | he is (he's) | she is (she's) |
| it is (it's) | we are (we're) | you are (you're) | they are (they're) |

Answer the questions. Use complete sentences. The first one is done for you.

1. What street is your school on? _It's on Main Street._ _____

2. What day is it today? _____

3. Are you tired today? _____

4. What is your last name? _____

5. What is your favorite color? _____

6. Are your shoes black? _____

7. Are you a twin? _____

8. Is English easy or difficult for you? _____

9. Where are your books? _____

10. Is your house big or small? _____

11. Are your friends young or old? _____

12. Is a new car cheap? _____

13. How old are you? _____

14. What time is it now? _____

15. What color are your eyes? _____

16. Are you tall or short? _____

17. Is your school beautiful or ugly? _____

18. What is your favorite school subject? _____

19. Who is your English teacher? _____

20. Is today a beautiful day? _____

21. Are cats large animals? _____

22. Where is your English class? _____

Skill Objective: Answering questions with present forms of *to be*. Review the present forms of the verb "to be" with all subject pronouns. Call attention to the abbreviations and point out that students can use either the full form or the abbreviated form. Do the first two questions orally with the class before assigning the page as independent work.

Stevie Wonder: Reading a Biography

Stevie Wonder is a singer and a song writer. He is from Michigan. Michigan is a state in the United States.

Stevie Wonder is famous all over the world, not just in the United States. People everywhere like his music.

Stevie Wonder is blind. He can not see. He is interested in computers. He has a special computer. His computer can read to him.

Stevie Wonder is a rich man now. He helps many sick people. He also helps people in many poor countries.

A. Answer the following questions about Stevie Wonder. The first one is done for you.

1. Is Stevie Wonder a newspaper writer? _No, he isn't._

2. Is Stevie Wonder from the United States? _____

3. Where is Michigan? _____

4. Is Stevie Wonder famous all over the world? _____

5. Why is Stevie Wonder famous? _____

_____

6. Is Stevie Wonder blind? _____

7. What can Stevie Wonder's computer do? _____

8. Is Stevie Wonder poor? _____

B. Read the sentences. Then circle the best answer.

Stevie Wonder is a rich and famous singer. He is also blind.
This shows that people who are blind or handicapped:

a. can sing very well.

b. cannot see very well.

c. can do almost everything other people can do.

d. need other people to help them all the time.

C. On your paper, write about a famous person you like. Tell where he or she is from. Tell what he or she is famous for. Tell any other information you know. Your teacher or your librarian can help you find out about the person.

D A T A B A N K

blind	handicapped	rich
computer	music	singer
famous	poor	writer

Skill Objectives: Reading a biography; making inferences; writing a paragraph. Read the story aloud and go over any vocabulary that may be new to the students. Ask them if they have heard Stevie Wonder or know any of his songs, such as "I Just Called to Say I Love You." *Part A:* Do the first two questions orally. *Part B:* Students need to understand the words *blind* and *handicapped* before they can make an inference about such people. *Part C:* "Famous persons" can include historical figures, other popular entertainers, or persons in the news.

Using Capital Letters

Capital letters are "large" letters. For example, the *B* in *Bob* is a capital letter. When you write, you need to use both capital and small letters. Here are some rules for using capital letters.

---

1. Use a capital letter for the first word in every sentence.
    Example: **T**he boy is sitting on the chair.

2. Use a capital letter for the first person singular (**I**).
    Example: My brother and **I** are going to Mexico.

3. Use a capital letter for names of people, days of the week, months of the year, cities, and countries.
    Example: **T**om is going to **N**ew **Y**ork on **M**onday, the 5th of **D**ecember.

4. Use a capital letter for the names of streets, schools, languages, and holidays.
    Example: The **E**nglish classes at the **A**dams **L**anguage **S**chool on **C**opley **S**treet start the day after **L**abor **D**ay.

On your own paper, rewrite the following sentences, capitalizing words where necessary.

1. her sister is living in japan.
2. i want to be an architect when i finish school.
3. mr johnson would like a carton of eggs at the store.
4. many schools begin classes in september in the united states.
5. november, december, and january are cold months in canada.
6. janet is talking with rosita perez, the principal.
7. mark and bill wear their green pants to work on saturdays.
8. gina is tall but i am short.
9. binh nguyen and his sister live on everett street.
10. we have a test in english this friday.
11. the flag of colombia is red, blue, and yellow.
12. columbus day is always on monday and always in october.
13. the capital of ohio is columbus and the capital of south carolina is columbia.
14. people in france celebrate bastille day every year in july.
15. boston university is on commonwealth avenue in boston, but boston college is on commonwealth avenue in newton.

Skill Objective: Following rules for capitalization. On the board, explain the difference between the capital and "small" letters. Go over the rule box, asking volunteers to read the four rules and asking other students to come up and write different examples of each rule. After ample practice, explain the directions, pass out paper (or have students open their notebooks), do the first sentence together and assign the remaining sentences as independent work.

Letters to a Friend

Dear Rosanna,
This is a picture of my boyfriend, Manuel. He's tall and thin and he's very handsome! His hair is black, and in this picture he's wearing a sweater and jeans.
Your friend,
Lisa

Dear Ben,
This is my new girlfriend. Her first name is Julia, her last name is Garcia. She is a Mexican American. Her mother is from Texas, and her father is from Acapulco. She's short. She's 14 and very friendly and pretty.
Your friend,
Carlos

Write a letter to a friend. Draw a picture of a boyfriend or girlfriend you like—a real person or a star.

Dear _____ ,

_____

_____

_____

_____

_____

_____ ,

_____

Skill Objectives: Describing; writing a friendly letter. Ask volunteers to read the two letters aloud. Have students note the placement and form of the greeting and closing and the indention of the first line of the letter. Have students suggest questions to be answered in the letters they are going to write: "What is your boyfriend's/girlfriend's name? What does he/she look like? How old is he/she?" After drawing a picture, students will write a letter describing their friend. The letters on the page will serve as models for form and content.

49

What's His Name?

Hi! My name is Manuel Rodriguez. At school, I am Manuel. At home, my name is Manolo. With my friends, I am Papo. With my basketball coach, I am Rodriguez. At work, I am Manny. I am a boy with many names!

A. What is his name with:

1. his math teacher? _____

2. his mother? _____

3. his sister? _____

4. his friend Pablo? _____

5. his coach? _____

6. his principal? _____

7. his boss? _____

8. his father? _____

B. What is this story mostly about? Circle the best answer.

Manuel and his family.

Manuel and his teachers.

Manuel and his names.

Manuel and his friends.

C. Are you a person with more than one name, too? Write a paragraph like Manny's.

Hi! My name is _____

_____

_____

_____

_____

_____

_____

Skill Objectives: Identifying main idea and details; writing a paragraph. Ask several students to give their full names and nicknames ("What does your family call you? What do your friends call you?" etc.) List the full names and nicknames on the board. Read the story aloud, or have students read it silently. *Part A:* Have students answer orally, then assign for writing. *Part B:* After students choose the main idea have them discuss why each choice is correct or incorrect. *Part C:* Students should model their paragraphs after the story at the top. (For paragraph format, they may also refer to the model paragraph on page 127.)

Dear Dot

Dear Dot—

I am a girl with long, dark hair and dark eyes, and so is my sister. My favorite color is blue, and so is my sister's. We are both tennis players. We are twins! We are happy being twins, but here is our problem. Boys don't know who is who, so they don't ask us out. They feel nervous and silly because they can't tell us apart. I'm staying home too many Friday nights, and so is my sister. What can we do?

Lonely Twin

1. How are the sisters alike? _____

_____

_____

2. What is their problem? _____

_____

3. Why do the boys feel nervous and silly? _____

_____

4. What is your advice for Lonely Twin? Circle your answer.
   a. Be different from your sister.
   b. Call up boys and ask them for dates.
   c. Wear a name tag.
   d. Go out alone on Friday nights.

5. Now read Dot's answer. See if your answer is the same. If your answer is different, tell why you disagree. Dot's advice is below.

Dear Lonely Twin—

You and your sister are too much alike. Change your hair style. Wear different colors. Play different sports. If that doesn't work, wear name tags!

Dot

Skill Objectives: Reading comprehension; making judgments. Read the letter aloud as students follow along. Explain any unfamiliar words. Ask students to reread the letter silently, then answer questions 1-4. Correct the first three answers, then let students compare their choice of advice. Read Dot's answer together. Let students say why they agree or disagree with Dot's reply and perhaps offer some other suggestions.

Food

A. Learn the words for the foods below. Find the words in the Data Bank, then write each word on the line.

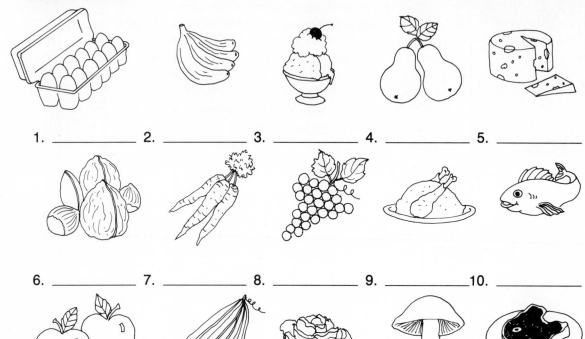

1. _____ 2. _____ 3. _____ 4. _____ 5. _____

6. _____ 7. _____ 8. _____ 9. _____ 10. _____

11. _____ 12. _____ 13. _____ 14. _____ 15. _____

B. Answer the following questions about the foods above. Circle the correct answer. The first one is done for you.

1. What food is red, yellow, or green?

   a fish   b. carrots   (c. apples)

2. What food is good for a sandwich?

   a. peanuts   b. cheese   c. ice cream

3. What food is from a chicken?

   a. beans   b. eggs   c. cheese

4. What food is long and orange?

   a. chicken   b. pears   c. carrots

5. What food is yellow and sweet?

   a. bananas   b. meat   c. grapes

D A T A   B A N K

apples	carrots	eggs	ice cream	mushrooms
bananas	cheese	fish	lettuce	nuts
beans	chicken	grapes	meat	pears

Skill Objectives: Learning food vocabulary; answering multiple choice questions. *Part A*: Introduce or review the vocabulary. Point out the plural forms used for items 1, 2, 4, 6, 7, 8, 11, 12, and call attention to the Data Bank at the bottom of the page where all fifteen answers will be found. *Part B*: Point out that these items are in another multiple choice format. Show how the first answer has been marked by circling "c. apples." Discuss why this answer is correct and why the others are not. Then assign the page for independent written work.

Doing Things

You can use *am, is,* or *are* plus a word with *-ing* to tell what someone is doing. Look at these sentences.

I am eating a steak.   We are eating eggs.   You are eating an apple.
She is drinking tea.   He is cooking fish.   They are buying ice cream.

A. Look at the pictures below. Write a sentence on the line to tell what the people or animals are doing. Use Data Bank A to help you. The first one is done for you.

1. *It is drinking.*   2. _____   3. _____

4. _____   5. _____   6. _____

D A T A   B A N K   A

| eating | drinking | cooking | buying |

B. What are these people doing? Write a sentence on the line. Use Data Bank B.

 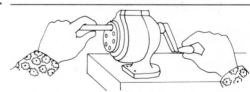

1. _____   2. _____

3. _____   4. _____

D A T A   B A N K   B

opening their books   sharpening her pencil
walking in the hall   paying attention to the teacher

Skill Objectives: Recognizing subject pronouns; present progressive tense. *Part A:* Call attention to picture 1 and ask, "What is the cat doing?" Have a volunteer read the sentence under the picture. Ask similar questions for pictures 2 through 6. Students are to use the correct pronoun and one of the words in Data Bank A for their answers. After all questions have been done orally, have students write their answers. *Part B:* Use a similar procedure. Students will use one of the phrases in Data Bank B for each item.

Hamburgers Unlimited!

Use a menu to find the costs of different meals.

Read the menu of Hamburgers Unlimited. Then do the exercises.

Regular hamburger	.89	Filet fish sandwich	1.63
Regular cheeseburger	1.15	Fried chicken sandwich	1.94
Double hamburger	1.79		
Double cheeseburger	1.99	Regular coffee or tea	.68
		Large coffee or tea	.88
Regular fries	.79	Regular milk	.68
Large fries	1.35	Large milk	.88
		Regular cola	.79
Milk Shakes (Vanilla, Chocolate,		Large cola	1.00
Strawberry) Regular	1.04	Regular diet cola	.79
Large	1.35	Large diet cola	1.00

A. Add up these bills. Are they correct?   Yes or No?

1. A regular hamburger, a regular fries, and a regular cola is $2.68.   _____

2. A double hamburger with a regular coffee is $2.47.   _____

3. A fish sandwich, a large fries, and a regular diet cola is $3.77.   _____

4. Two cheeseburgers, a large fries, and a large coffee is $3.63.   _____

5. A fried chicken sandwich and a strawberry milk shake is $2.77.   _____

6. A double cheeseburger, a fish sandwich, a regular chocolate shake, and a large cola is $5.66.   _____

B. You are at Hamburgers Unlimited! Practice this conversation with a classmate.

—What would you like?

—I'd like _____ , please.

—Anything to drink with that?

—Yes, I'd like _____ .

—That's $ _____ .

—Thank you.

—You're welcome.

C. On your own paper, write about your favorite kind of "fast food" (hamburgers, hot dogs, fried chicken, pizza, etc.). Tell why you like it.

Skill Objectives: Practicing money skills; using a chart. *Part A:* Discuss the menu with the class. Then ask a student to place his/her order. Say, "Can I help you?" If necessary, add "Anything to drink?" after the student has ordered. Write the student's order on the board. Have the class find the price of each item, then calculate the total bill. Repeat several times, then assign Part A for independent work. *Part B:* Allow time for students to role play; circulate and provide help if necessary. *Part C:* Discuss different kinds of fast food and which ones students prefer. Then have them write about their favorite.

More Food

1. sausage
2. lobster
3. black beans
4. strawberries
5. shrimps

6. clams
7. hamburger
8. spare ribs
9. pork chops
10. melon

11. tomatoes
12. onions
13. cherries
14. rice
15. peppers

16. tuna
17. roast beef
18. corn
19. cucumbers
20. potatoes

Look at the pictures of the foods above. Then look at the names of the four food groups below. Decide which group each food belongs in and write its name under the heading for that group. The first one is done for you.

MEAT	SEAFOOD	VEGETABLES	FRUITS
sausage			

Skill Objectives: Building vocabulary; classifying. Let volunteers name familiar food pictures. Then teach the new vocabulary items. Play a cumulative list game for vocabulary reinforcement. Student A will say, "I am eating (pork chops) for dinner." The next student will repeat that food and add a food of his/her own: "I am eating pork chops and (sausage) for dinner." Students do not have to limit themselves to the foods on this page. Call attention to the chart at the bottom of the page. Work as a group to classify the first few foods. Then let students complete the chart independently.

In the Cafeteria

Use information in a dialogue to help you make inferences.

It's lunch time at Roosevelt High School. Binh, Rosa, and Tom are waiting in line.

TOM: What's for lunch today?
ROSA: I think it's pizza.
BINH: I hope so. I love pizza.
TOM: Not me. I don't like pizza. I like tacos.
ROSA: I'm not very hungry. I only want a salad.

Now Binh, Rosa, and Tom are at the front of the line. Mrs. May is serving lunch.

BINH: What's for lunch, Mrs. May?
MRS. MAY: Fried chicken.
ROSA: I'll have that.
TOM: Me too.
BINH: The same for me.

Mrs. May smiles and gives the students their lunch.

A. Answer the questions about the dialogue. Fill in the circles.

1. Where do the students go to school?
   a. in the cafeteria
   b. for pizza
   c. at Roosevelt High School

   ⓐ ⓑ ⓒ

2. What food does Binh love?
   a. pizza
   b. tacos
   c. salad

   ⓐ ⓑ ⓒ

3. What does Tom say about pizza?
   a. He's eating it for lunch.
   b. He isn't hungry for pizza.
   c. He doesn't like it.

   ⓐ ⓑ ⓒ

4. Who is Mrs. May?
   a. a teacher at the school
   b. Tom's mother
   c. a cafeteria worker

   ⓐ ⓑ ⓒ

5. Which of the following is true about the students
   in the dialogue?
   a. They like pizza.
   b. They want salads.
   c. They like fried chicken.

   ⓐ ⓑ ⓒ

B. Make a chart with two columns on your paper like the one you see here. Complete the chart with your own food likes and dislikes.

Food I Like	Food I Don't Like

Skill Objective: Using information to make inferences. *Part A:* Do question 1 orally with the class to be sure students remember how to mark their answers. *Part B:* Students can use the vocabulary from pages 52, 54, and 55 in making their lists.

Buying Food

A. Write the words. The first one is done for you.

1. ___a can of tuna___

2. _____

3. _____

4. _____

5. _____

6. _____

7. _____

8. _____

9. _____

10. _____

11. _____

12. _____

D A T A B A N K

a carton of eggs	a head of lettuce	a can of tuna
a box of cereal	a bag of onions	a bottle of oil
a quart of juice	a gallon of milk	a jar of peanut butter
a pound of hamburg	a bunch of carrots	a loaf of bread

B. Odd Man Out: Circle the word that does not belong. The first one is done for you.

1. hamburger, (lettuce) sausage, roast beef.
2. large, small, medium, first.
3. coffee, fish, milk, lemonade.
4. picture, drug store, school, restaurant.
5. near, across, is, in.
6. bed, table, shoe, chair.
7. eggs, box, can, jar.
8. second, three o'clock, ten thirty, quarter of one.
9. tall, old, fat, man.
10. bacon, eggs, toast, ice cream.

Skill Objectives: Building vocabulary; reviewing food vocabulary; classifying. *Part A:* If possible bring in a variety of groceries to teach vocabulary. Include boxes, bags, cans, quart containers, etc. Have students locate the weight or capacity on the container. Have them list other goods that are packed in cans, boxes, etc. Teach or review the vocabulary on the page, go over the instructions for Part A and assign it for independent work. *Part B:* "Odd Man Out" is a classifying activity. Ask for volunteers to tell why *lettuce* is circled in the first item. Do a few more examples orally, then assign for independent work.

A or An?

Use AN before a vowel (a,e,i,o,u) or a vowel sound.

    an apple   an egg   an hour   an honest man

Use A before a consonant (b,c,d,f,g,h,j,k,l,m,n,p,q,r,s,t,v,w,x,y,z) or a consonant-sounding vowel.

    a banana   a used car   a teacher   a yellow box

Fill in with *A* or *AN*. Then practice reading the sentences aloud with a friend.

1. He is reading _____*an*_____ English book.

2. Lisa is _____ pretty girl.

3. Tom is eating _____ apple.

4. Mrs. Thompson is _____ old woman.

5. Maria is buying _____ banana and _____ pear.

6. James is studying at _____ university in New York.

7. Luis is eating _____ orange.

8. Mrs. Lee is wearing _____ red dress.

9. My father is _____ honest man.

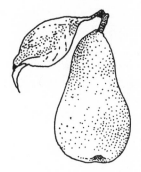

10. She is eating _____ egg for breakfast.

11. Paul is looking at _____ new car.

12. David is _____ thin boy.

13. The baby is eating _____ ice cream cone.

14. The boy is buying _____ umbrella.

15. Sandra is wearing _____ orange coat.

16. Michael is wearing _____ blue shirt.

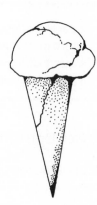

17. Sally is _____ eight year old girl.

18. Mr. Jones is _____ happy man.

19. The boy is eating _____ carrot.

20. Jack is sitting on _____ chair.

Skill Objective: Using articles a *and* an. Go over the rules at the top of the page with the class. Point out that *an* is used in words beginning with a silent *h: an hour, an honest man.* The article *a* is used before words beginning with a long *u: a used car.* Practice the examples and other words orally before assigning the page for independent and pair work.

Questions with "Like"

Many students are confused by questions with the word "like." Look at the following box.

"Like" question	Explanation	Possible Answer
"What would you like?"	This means the same as "What do you want?"	"I would like a pizza."
"What sports do you like?"	This means the same as "What sports are your favorites?"	"I like hockey and soccer."
"What do you look like?"	This means the same as "How do you describe yourself?"	"I'm tall with black hair and blue eyes." (Notice that "look like is not part of the answer.)

A. Now read the following story and answer the questions.

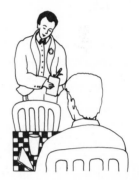

John Perry is in a restaurant. He is hungry and he would like to eat a big dinner. He calls the waiter. He says, "I'd like a steak, french fries, and a large salad." John Perry is an athlete. He is 6 feet tall and weighs 170 pounds. He has blond hair and brown eyes. John is so hungry because he played sports all day. In the morning he played basketball. In the afternoon he played soccer. Those are his favorite sports.

1. What does John Perry look like? _____

_____

2. What would John like to eat? _____

_____

3. What sports does John like to play? _____

_____

B. What about you? Answer the following questions on a separate sheet of paper.

1. What do you look like?
2. What sports do you like?
3. What would you like to eat for dinner tonight?

Ask 5 other people these 3 questions. Write down their answers.

Skill Objective: Differentiating among uses of *like*. Before assigning the page, prepare several additional examples of each "like" meaning to be sure students understand the difference. *Part A:* Read the paragraph orally together and go over any new vocabulary. Then do question 1 orally with the class. *Part B:* Discuss the three questions. Then have students write answers about themselves. Have them interview five others, using the same questions and writing these persons' answers. As an extension, you may wish to have the class chart the results of their interviews.

Dear Dot

Dear Dot—

My mother is on a diet. My sister is on a diet. My grandmother is on a diet. I am NOT on a diet, and there is nothing good to eat in my house. I like steak and pork chops, potatoes and rice. I want an ice cream or a pizza <u>NOW</u>! My mother is eating only salad and fish. My sister is eating only carrots, cucumbers, and tomatoes. My grandmother is eating only chicken and lettuce. I am STARVING! What can I do?

A Hungry Boy

1. Who is on a diet? _____

_____

2. What does the boy like? _____

_____

3. What is his mother eating? _____

_____

4. What is his sister eating? _____

_____

5. What is his grandmother eating? _____

6. What is your advice for Hungry Boy? Circle your answer.

   a. Go on a diet too.   c. Go to a restaurant to eat every night.

   b. Eat only candy; don't eat at home.   d. Eat diet meals at home and other food outside.

7. Now read Dot's answer. See if your answer is the same. If your answer is different, tell why you disagree. Dot's advice is below.

Dear Hungry—

Eat at a friend's house. Eat the food you like at lunch. Learn to like salad and fish and chicken. Buy some snacks and eat them before you go home. But be careful! You don't want to be on a diet too.

Dot

Skill Objectives: Reading comprehension; making judgments. Have students recall the previous "Dear Dot" page (page 51). Read Hungry Boy's letter aloud as students follow along. Explain any unfamiliar words. Ask students to reread the letter silently, then answer questions 1–6. Correct the first five answers, then let students compare their choice of advice. Read Dot's answer together. Let students tell why they agree or disagree with Dot's reply and perhaps offer some other solutions.

60

Families

This is the Peterson family.

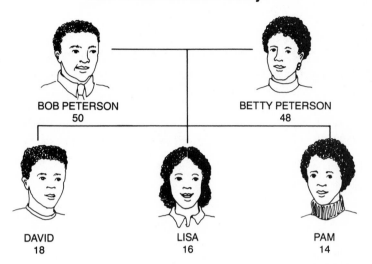

BOB PETERSON
50

BETTY PETERSON
48

DAVID
18

LISA
16

PAM
14

Bob and Betty Peterson are married. Betty is Bob's wife. Bob is Betty's husband. Betty and Bob are parents of three children. David is 18 years old. David is Bob and Betty's son. Lisa and Pam are Bob and Betty's daughters. David is Lisa and Pam's brother. Lisa and Pam are David's sisters. Bob is their father. Betty is their mother.

A. Answer these questions. The first one is done for you.

1. Who is the husband? _____Bob_____

2. Who is the wife? _____

3. Who are the parents? _____

4. Who is the son? _____

5. Who are the daughters? _____

6. Who are the children? _____

7. Who are David's sisters? _____

8. Who is Pam and Lisa's brother? _____

B. Answer "yes" or "no" to the following statements.

___No__ 1. Bob is married to Pam.

_____ 2. Bob and Betty are the parents of three children.

_____ 3. Pam and Lisa are brothers.

_____ 4. David is Bob and Betty's daughter.

_____ 5. David is the father.

_____ 6. Bob Peterson is fifty years old.

_____ 7. David, Lisa, and Betty are the children.

_____ 8. Betty and Pam are sisters.

D A T A   B A N K

family	parents	father	husband	daughter	children
mother	married	son	sister	wife	brother

Skill Objectives: Building vocabulary; answering questions. Teach or review the vocabulary on the page. Read the story about the Peterson family aloud. *Part A*: Work through the first three questions orally with the class. Then assign Part A as independent work. *Part B*: Remind students to write *Yes* or *No* for each statement in Part B.

61

Amy's Family

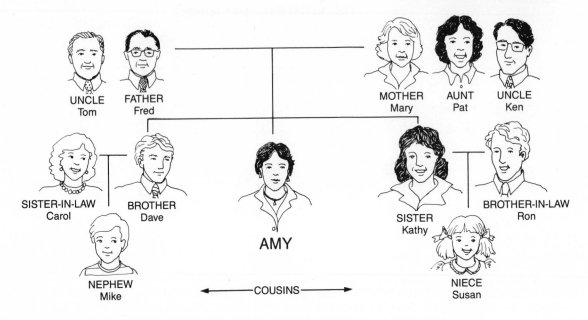

A. Explain these person's relationships to Amy. The first one is done for you.

1. Kathy _She's Amy's sister._

2. Mike _____

3. Fred _____

4. Ron _____

5. Pat _____

6. Susan _____

7. Ken _____

8. Tom _____

B. That's not right! Complete the "no" answers with an explanation.

1. Is Carol Amy's sister? _No, she's Amy's sister-in-law._

2. Is Mary Amy's aunt? _No,_____

3. Is Pat Mary's cousin? _No,_____

4. Is Susan Carol's daughter? _No,_____

5. Is Tom Fred's father? _No,_____

6. Is Mike Susan's brother? _No,_____

7. Is Ron Susan's uncle? _No,_____

8. Is Tom Pat's uncle? _No,_____

Skill Objectives: Building vocabulary; understanding a "family tree" chart. Examine the family chart with the students. Ask questions about each person. Review such familiar terms as *brother* and introduce new terms such as *sister-in-law*. Ask, "Who is Amy's sister-in-law? To whom is she married?" *Part A:* Work through the first four items orally before assigning Part A for independent written work. *Part B:* Make sure students understand that the answer to all the questions is "No," and that they must tell what the relationship actually is. Do the first four items orally with the class, then assign Part B for written work.

Mr., Mrs., Miss, and Ms.

Many students are confused by the titles Mr., Mrs., Miss, and Ms. Read the explanation in the box.

Mr. (pronounced mis' ter) always refers to a man, married or single (not married).

Mrs. (pronounced miss' is) refers to a married woman (or one who was married).

Miss refers to a single woman (a woman who is not married and was never married).

Ms. (pronounced mizz) refers to any woman, married or single.

A. Look at the following names. Circle *male* if the person is a male (man) or *female* if the person is a female (a woman). Circle *M* if the person is married or *S* if the person is single. Circle *?* if it is not possible to tell if the person is married or single.

1. Mr. Jamie Sullivan   male / female   S   M   ?
2. Mrs. John Jones   male / female   S   M   ?
3. Miss Pat Wu   male / female   S   M   ?
4. Mr. Tracey Rogers   male / female   S   M   ?
5. Ms. M.L. West   male / female   S   M   ?
6. Mrs. P.X. Kennedy   male / female   S   M   ?
7. Ms. Jordan Karr   male / female   S   M   ?
8. Miss Dana Dorland   male / female   S   M   ?

B. Write the names of some males and females you know. Use name titles, for example, Mr. Liem Nguyen, or Miss Melida Muñoz.

Males	Females
_____	_____
_____	_____
_____	_____
_____	_____
_____	_____
_____	_____

C. Some women prefer to be called Miss or Mrs. Some prefer to be called Ms. Talk about this with some of your friends. Then write on another sheet of paper why you think a woman might choose to be called Ms. instead of Miss or Mrs.

Skill Objective: Learning, pronouncing, distinguishing among different name titles. Go over the information in the box with the students, and answer questions. *Part A:* Work through the first two examples with the class. Be sure students understand the terms *male* and *female*. As students volunteer answers for the first column (male/female), ask, "How do you know?" Do the same with the second column (S, M, ?). *Part B:* You may wish to have students use the names of classmates or family members. Check to be sure they understand the directions. *Part C:* Assign to students who need challenge. You may wish to use it only as a discussion question.

Where Are They?

A. Answer the questions. The first one is done for you.

1. Are you in the bedroom?

No, I'm not.

I'm in the kitchen.

2. Is the cat in the yard?

_____

_____

3. Is Cathy on her bike?

_____

_____

4. Is Tom under the car?

_____

_____

B. Write the questions.

1. _____

   _____

No, they aren't.

They're in the bathtub.

2. _____

   _____

No, we aren't.

We're in front of the fireplace.

3. _____

   _____

No, he isn't.

He's behind the tree.

4. _____

   _____

No, they aren't.

They're under the bed.

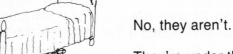

Skill Objectives: Forming contractions; reviewing prepositions. Set classroom objects on a desk. Example: a stack of different colored books, an eraser behind the books, a box with pencils in front of the books. Ask questions beginning "Is/Are . . .?" ("Are the books under the desk?") Students should answer with a negative contraction, then give the correct information using a pronoun contraction. ("No, they aren't. They're on the desk.") Encourage students to ask each other questions. Work orally, then assign the page for independent work.

Bill's Apartment Building

Use a picture to help you describe a building.

A. Write the answers. Use *on* or *in*.

1. Where is the lobby?

   It's on the first floor.

2. Where is the laundry room?

   _____

3. Where is Bill's apartment?

   _____

4. Where is the T.V. antenna?

   _____

5. Where is the balcony?

   _____

6. Where is the manager's office?

   _____

7. Where is Mrs. Doe's apartment?

   _____

8. Where is the store room?

   _____

B. Bill's apartment has four rooms. What is in each room? Use the Data Bank to fill in the chart. You may write each word more than once.

Living room	Kitchen	Bedroom	Bathroom

D A T A   B A N K

armchair	chair	mirror	shower	stove	toilet
bathtub	dresser	refrigerator	sink	table	TV
bed	lamp	rug	sofa		

Skill Objectives: Building vocabulary; classifying. *Part A:* Discuss the apartment building. Establish that there are three floors and a basement. Ask, "What's on the first floor? Where is the laundry room?" etc. Listen for correct use of *in* and *on*. Ask students, "Do you live in an apartment building? What floor do you live on? What rooms do you have in your apartment?" Go over the questions orally before assigning them as written work. *Part B:* Teach/review the vocabulary in the Data Bank. Categorize the first few items as a group, then assign as independent work.

What Are They Doing?

I am working.	He She } is working. It	You We } are working. They

Write a sentence to go with each picture. Use the model above as a guide. The first one is done for you.

1. *He is writing.*   2. _____   3. _____

4. _____   5. _____   6. _____

7. _____   8. _____   9. _____

10. _____   11. _____   12. _____

DATA BANK

watching	reading	shopping	driving	running	eating
dancing	riding	writing	sleeping	playing	washing

Skill Objective: Practicing the present progressive tense. Teach/review the vocabulary in the Data Bank. Have each verb pronounced. If there is confusion about the meaning of any verb, ask volunteers to act that verb out. Then go through the page orally. Other volunteers can suggest sentences for each picture, using the sample sentence under the first picture as a model. Monitor answers for correct subject pronouns. After sufficient oral practice, assign the page as written work.

66

Spell-ING

A. Read the box below.

> There are a few rules to follow when you add *-ing* to a word.
>
> **Rule 1.** For most words add *-ing* with no changes. Example: walk–walking.
>
> **Rule 2.** For words that end in silent (not pronounced) *e,* drop the *e* and add *-ing.* Example: dance–dancing.
>
> **Rule 3.** For one-syllable words that end in consonant–vowel–consonant (except x, w, and l), double the last letter and add *-ing.* Example: sit–sitting.

B. Add *-ing* to each of the words below. All of the words are from pages in this book. They are words you know already. Follow the rules.

Rule 1–Add *-ing* with no change.

1. talk _____
2. open _____
3. wear _____
4. eat _____
5. wait _____

6. shout _____
7. call _____
8. buy _____
9. listen _____
10. study _____

Rule 2–Drop the final *e* and add *-ing.*

11. come _____
12. erase _____
13. give _____
14. take _____
15. drive _____

16. raise _____
17. live _____
18. write _____
19. ride _____
20. type _____

Rule 3–Double the final consonant and add *-ing.*

21. run _____
22. shop _____
23. stop _____

24. get _____
25. spot _____
26. hit _____

C. Now write a sentence for each *-ing* word. Example: He is talking to the teacher.

Skill Objective: Learning spelling rules for adding *-ing*. *Part A:* Read over the box with the students. Add several more examples for each rule. (Try to avoid using the verbs in Part B.) Make sure that students understand the concept of "silent *e*," and that they understand what a one-syllable consonant-vowel-consonant verb is. *Part B:* Do one or two examples for each rule with the class, then assign as written work. *Part C:* After students have written their sentences, ask each one to read his/her favorite sentence to the class.

The Kent Family at Home

Here are some questions about the Kent family. There are three answers after each question. Read all three answers. Decide which is the best answer and fill in the correct circle. The first one is done for you.

1. Where is Mr. Kent?   Ⓐ ● Ⓒ
   a. He's in the garage.
   b. He's in the kitchen.
   c. He's in the yard.

2. What is he doing?   Ⓐ Ⓑ Ⓒ
   a. He's cooking dinner.
   b. He's watching TV.
   c. He's playing tennis.

3. Are the pets in the house?   Ⓐ Ⓑ Ⓒ
   a. The dog is in the house.
   b. No, they aren't.
   c. They are sleeping.

4. Where is Mrs. Kent?   Ⓐ Ⓑ Ⓒ
   a. She's in the yard.
   b. She's in the kitchen.
   c. She's in the living room.

5. What is Mrs. Kent doing?   Ⓐ Ⓑ Ⓒ
   a. She's cooking.
   b. She's reading a book.
   c. She's eating dinner.

6. Where are the boys?   Ⓐ Ⓑ Ⓒ
   a. They are in the kitchen.
   b. They are in the living room.
   c. They are in the yard.

7. Where are the girls?   Ⓐ Ⓑ Ⓒ
   a. They are in the bedroom.
   b. They are in the kitchen.
   c. They are in the yard.

8. What are they doing?   Ⓐ Ⓑ Ⓒ
   a. They are washing the car.
   b. They are doing homework.
   c. They are listening to music.

Skill Objectives: Present progressive; reviewing vocabulary; answering multiple choice questions. Discuss the picture with the class. Ask questions such as "How many daughters/sons do Mr. and Mrs. Kent have? Where are they? What are they doing?" After sufficient oral practice, go over question 1 to be sure students understand the directions before assigning the page as independent written work.

Two Families

Read and write about families.

Each year, many young people come to the United States from other countries. You are going to read about two of these young people and their families.

A. Sue-Ling's Family

Hello! My name is Sue-Ling. I'm 15, and I'm from Hong Kong. I am a student, and I'm in the tenth grade at South High School. I like school. My favorite subjects are math and art.

I'm living here in Chicago with my family. My father is a chef in a restaurant. My mother works at the restaurant part-time. I have two younger brothers, Jing, 6, and Ho, 9. They are in elementary school. I love my family.

Now read each sentence. Write "T" if the sentence is true. Write "F" if it is false. Write "?" if the story doesn't tell you the answer. The first two are done for you.

_T_ 1. The girl's name is Sue-Ling.

_?_ 2. Her mother's name is Wei-Ming.

____ 3. Sue-Ling is from Japan.

____ 4. She is a chef.

____ 5. Her mother likes her job.

____ 6. Her mother works ten hours a week.

____ 7. Her brothers are younger than she is.

____ 8. Her father is fifty years old.

____ 9. She is living in Hong Kong.

____ 10. Sue-Ling likes math and art.

B. Roberto's Family

Write one word in each space to complete the story of Roberto's family.

Hello! My name is Roberto Ruiz. I ____*am*____ from El Salvador. El Salvador _____ a country in Central America. I am 14, and I am living _____ Miami, Florida, with my family.

My father _____ a teacher. He teaches Spanish at Stewart High School. My mother _____ a housewife, but she is _____ part time at a factory. My sisters, Carmen and Rosita, _____ both ten years old. They _____ twins! They attend elementary school. My brother, Raul, is _____ college. He _____ studying computer science. I love my family.

C. Write a paragraph about your own family.

Skill Objectives: Answering true-false-? questions; completing a cloze exercise; writing a paragraph. *Part A:* Read the story of Sue Ling aloud as the students follow along. Ask true/false questions about the story. Then ask one or two questions that the students can't possibly answer from the facts in the story, so they understand the "?" component. The first two statements are already marked: go through them to be sure students understand why these answers are correct. Do several other items orally before assigning Part A for independent work. *Part B:* Be sure students understand what to do. You may wish to do the whole exercise orally before having students do it in writing.

Writing Questions

Read this paragraph about Robert's neighborhood.

It's a sunny Saturday, and everyone in Robert's neighborhood is outside today. Robert is riding his new bicycle. His next-door neighbor, David, is washing his car in the driveway. David's father is mowing the lawn. His other neighbors, Bill and Teddy, are playing ball in their yard. Their parents are playing ball, too. It's a nice day to be outside!

A. Write yes/no questions about the paragraph. Use the verb "to be." See the model below. The first one is done for you.

Am I busy?	Is $\begin{matrix} he \\ she \\ it \end{matrix} \Big\}$ busy?	Are $\begin{matrix} you \\ we \\ they \end{matrix} \Big\}$ busy?

1. _Is it Saturday_____? Yes, it is.

2. _____? No, everyone is outside.

3. _____? No, David isn't his brother.

4. _____? Yes, he's in the driveway.

5. _____? Yes, he is. (David's father is at home.)

6. _____? No, they are in the yard.

7. _____? Yes, it is.

8. _____? No, I am not.

B. Write yes/no questions using the present progressive (-ing) form. See the model.

Am I working?	Is $\begin{matrix} he \\ she \\ it \end{matrix} \Big\}$ working?	Are $\begin{matrix} you \\ we \\ they \end{matrix} \Big\}$ working?

1. _____? No, he's riding his bicycle.

2. _____? Yes, he is. (He's washing his car.)

3. _____? No, he's mowing the lawn.

4. _____? Yes, they are. (They're playing ball.)

5. _____? Yes, they are playing with them.

Skill Objectives: Asking questions using _to be_; present progressive. Read the story about Robert's neighborhood aloud with the class. _Part A_: Discuss the models in the box. Then go through the eight items orally before having students write the questions. _Part B_: Discuss the models in the box. Work through the items orally before having students write the questions.

Dear Dot

Dear Dot—

My problem is, my father is never home. He is a sales representative, and he is always going to the airport or the train station or the bus station. He is working in Los Angeles this week. Next week he is going to Chicago. When my father _is_ at home, he is tired, or he is working in his office. What can I do?

Lonely Son

1. What's the boy's problem? _____

_____

2. What's his father's occupation? _____

_____

3. What's his father doing this week? _____

_____

4. Where is his father going next week? _____

_____

5. What is your advice for Lonely Son?

   a. Don't bother your father.   c. Talk with your father about your feelings.

   b. Become a salesman too.   d. Surprise your father and meet him in Chicago.

6. Now read Dot's answer. See if your answer is the same. If your answer is different, tell why you disagree. Dot's advice is below.

Dear Lonely Son—

Many young people write to me with the same problem. Fathers and mothers are working hard and spending less time with their children. Talk to your father; tell him you want to spend more time with him. Maybe you can go with him on a short trip. Tell him you want to do things with him on the weekends. Remember, he's working hard to take care of you.

Dot

Skill Objectives: Reading comprehension; making judgments. Read the letter aloud as students follow along. Explain any unfamiliar words. Ask students to reread the letter silently, then answer questions 1-5. Correct the first four answers, then let students compare their choice of advice. Read Dot's answer together. Let students tell why they agree or disagree with Dot's solution and perhaps offer some other solutions.

71

Occupations

Look at each picture. Learn the job name. Then write what the people do, using the simple present tense. Use the Data Bank to help you.

Forms of the Simple Present Tense

I You We They } work.	I *work* at a restaurant. You *study* English. We *teach* English. They *fix* cars.

1. I'm a musician.

I play in an

orchestra.

2. I'm a pilot.

3. I'm a builder.

4. We are waiters.

5. We are mechanics.

6. We are nurses.

7. They are architects.

8. They are mail carriers.

9. They are custodians.

ⓓⒶⓉⒶ ⒷⒶⓃⓀ

We serve food in a restaurant.	We take care of sick people.	They deliver mail to homes.
They draw plans for buildings.	I fly airplanes.	They clean school buildings.
I build houses.	I play in an orchestra.	We fix cars and trucks.

Skill Objectives: Building vocabulary; using simple present tense. Teach/review the vocabulary and call attention to the box at the top of the page. Then have volunteers make sentences for each of the nine items. Call attention to the Data Bank before assigning this as independent work.

More Occupations

Look at each picture. Learn the job name. Then write what the people do, using the simple present tense. Use the Data Bank to help you.

More Forms of the Simple Present Tense		
He She It } works	(When the subject is *he, she,* or *it* or the name of a person or thing, add -s or -es to the verb.)	He *works* in a shop. It *rains* every spring. Jan *fixes* cars.

1. He is a reporter.
He writes stories for newspapers and T.V.

2. She is a farmer.
_____

3. He is a teacher.
_____

4. She is a photographer.
_____

5. He is a chef.
_____

6. She is a veterinarian.
_____

7. She is a police officer.
_____

8. He is an artist.
_____

9. She is a bus driver.
_____

D A T A   B A N K

drives a bus
cooks in a restaurant
teaches math

writes stories for newspapers and T.V.
takes pictures with a camera
grows food for people to eat

takes care of sick animals
draws and paints pictures
gives traffic tickets

Skill Objectives: Building vocabulary; using simple present tense. Call attention to the box at the top of the page and give several examples of the spelling and pronunciation of the *s/es* forms. You may want to devise a list of verbs with different *s/z/es* endings, such as *drives (z)*, *paints (s)*, and *watches (es)*. Teach/review the vocabulary, then have volunteers do the nine items orally. Monitor for correct pronunciation of verb endings. Call attention to the Data Bank. Then assign the page for independent written work.

73

A Working Family

Use a story to help you answer questions about people. Learn about more occupations.

The Wilsons are a busy family. Mr. Wilson is a chef. Mrs. Wilson is a police officer. John Wilson, their oldest son, is a dentist. His brother, Pete Wilson, is a construction worker.

Wendy Wilson, the Wilson's young daughter, is a student, but she works too. She works part time as a secretary.

Mr. Leone, Mrs. Wilson's father, lives with the family. He's retired. He's not a mail carrier any more. "I'm glad to stay home and rest my feet," says Mr. Leone. "I help my busy children and grandchildren whenever I can."

A. Answer the following questions. Circle your answers.

1. Who in the Wilson family works in a restaurant?

   a. Mr. Wilson   b. Mrs. Wilson   c. Wendy Wilson

2. Who in the Wilson family arrests criminals and gives tickets?

   a. Pete   b. John   c. Mrs. Wilson

3. Who pulls and fills teeth?

   a. John   b. Mr. Wilson   c. Mr. Leone

4. Who in the Wilson family builds buildings?

   a. Mr. Leone   b. Mr. Wilson   c. Pete Wilson

5. Who goes to school and works?

   a. Mrs. Wilson   b. Wendy Wilson   c. Pete Wilson

6. What is true about Mr. Leone?

   a. He is a mail carrier.   c. He is a nice man.

   b. He is a chef at a restaurant.

B. Read about the following people. Write the names of their jobs. Use the Data Bank to help you.

1. I take pictures for newspapers and magazines. _____

2. I help people when they have problems in court. _____

3. I fix water pipes in the kitchen and bathroom. _____

4. I put in electrical wiring and switches. _____

D A T A   B A N K

| lawyer | plumber | photographer | electrician |

Skill Objectives: Building vocabulary; making inferences. Have students read the story aloud. *Part A:* Do question 1 orally with the class. Ask them to tell why "Mr. Wilson" is the answer. Then assign Part A for independent work. After the class has finished marking their answers, correct Part A, asking for reasons for each choice. *Part B:* Review the vocabulary in the Data Bank, then ask students to write their answers. Discuss what other things people in each occupation do (for example, lawyers make wills, plumbers fix drains, photographers take portraits, electricians put in new lights and outlets).

How Much Do They Make?

This graph shows the approximate average annual salaries for people in various jobs. Be sure you understand the meanings of *approximate*, *average*, and *annual*. Read the graph and then do the exercises below it.

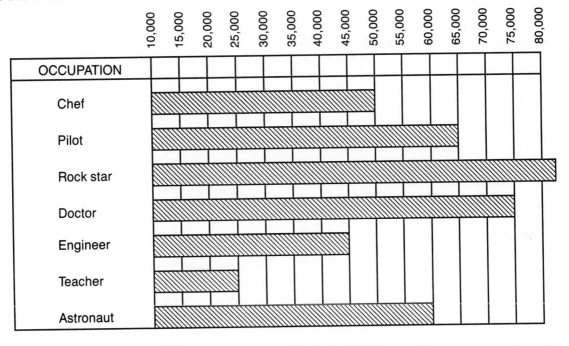

A. Read the sentences below carefully and fill in the blanks. The first one is done for you.

1. The approximate average salary for engineers is $___45,000___ a year.

2. Pilots are paid about $_____ a year.

3. The average doctor earns about $_____ annually.

4. Astronauts get paid approximately $_____ each year.

5. The average annual pay for teachers is around $_____ .

6. Chefs in restaurants have an annual salary of about $_____ .

7. Rock stars receive more than $_____ each year.

B. Read these sentences. Answer with YES or NO.

1. A teacher's average salary is more than a chef's.   _____
2. A doctor's salary is about $75,000 a year.   _____
3. Astronauts and doctors have about the same average salaries. _____
4. An engineer's average salary is less than a teacher's.   _____
5. The average annual salary of rock stars is more than $80,000. _____
6. A chef's average salary is about $50,000 a year.   _____

Skill Objectives: Reading a bar graph; understanding *more than, less than*. Read the directions aloud. Explain any unfamiliar words. Go over the data shown on the graph. For each occupation, ask, "What is the . . .'s salary?" *Part A:* Do the first example with the students. Show how the answer is read from the graph. Then assign the remaining items. *Part B:* Teach the phrases and concepts *more than* and *less than*. Ask, "Which salaries are more/less than the (pilot's) salary?" After sufficient oral practice, assign Part B for independent work. Correct and discuss the page with the class. If appropriate, have students research other salaries and graph them.

75

Interviewing:
Personal Preferences

A. Interview people in your school. Ask these questions. Write their answers in the chart.

What's your name?

How old are you?

What do you want to be?

What's your favorite song?

What's your favorite color?

What's your favorite food?

Name	Age	Occupation	Favorite Song	Favorite Color	Favorite Food

B. Write a paragraph about some of the people above.

_____

_____

_____

_____

_____

_____

_____

_____

Skill Objectives: Using a chart; writing a paragraph. Draw the chart from Part A on the board. Have students ask one volunteer the questions from the top of the page. Show students how to fill out their own charts. Repeat this activity, then allow time for students to interview and chart independently. *Part B:* Have students help you build a paragraph, using the information from the board chart. Example: *Linda is fifteen years old. She wants to be a pilot. Her favorite song is "Memories." Her favorite color is blue. Her favorite food is pizza.* You may wish to have students review the sample paragraph on page 127 before they write their own.

Where Are You From?

A. Match the countries and nationalities. Write the letter of the nationality name next to the name of the country it goes with. The first one is done for you.

Country

1. England   _j_
2. Ireland   _____
3. Laos   _____
4. Japan   _____
5. Canada   _____
6. Peru   _____
7. Mexico   _____
8. Vietnam   _____
9. United States   _____
10. Colombia   _____
11. Brazil   _____
12. Turkey   _____
13. China   _____
14. Puerto Rico   _____
15. Spain   _____
16. Lebanon   _____
17. Thailand   _____
18. India   _____
19. Switzerland   _____
20. Greece   _____

Nationality

a. Peruvian
b. Brazilian
c. Swiss
d. Puerto Rican
e. Vietnamese
f. Turkish
g. Lebanese
h. Japanese
i. Thai
j. English
k. Indian
l. American
m. Mexican
n. Chinese
o. Laotian
p. Greek
q. Irish
r. Spanish
s. Canadian
t. Colombian

B. Fill in the chart with any information you want. Then, on your own paper, write sentences about these people. See the example below.

Amin is from Lebanon. His native language is Arabic. He is a banker. He is 36 years old.

Name	Amin	Maria	Sue-Ling	Cristos	Hiro/Yoko	My Teacher	I
Country	Lebanon		China		Japan	?	?
Language	Arabic	Spanish		Greek			
Occupation	banker		chemist				
Age	36				22/24		

Skill Objectives: Naming countries and nationalities; completing a chart. Display a world map. Have students locate each country listed in Part A. Then ask, "What do we call people from (Vietnam)?" "Is anyone in this class from Vietnam?" ("Yes, Binh is Vietnamese.") Provide vocabulary as needed for students whose countries are not listed. *Part B*: Students are to fill in the missing information with any appropriate words. Do "Maria" with the class; then have the class write a sentence about her. When you are sure students understand the instructions, assign the page for independent work.

The Right Career

João Mendes is Cape Verdean. He is from Cape Verde, an island country near Africa in the Atlantic Ocean. João lives in the United States now, in New York City.

João works in a supermarket. He wants to be an accountant. He likes taking care of money problems. He is very careful with the money he makes at his job in the supermarket. He is saving so he can go to college. "I don't want to be a cashier forever," says João. "I know if I work hard and study hard, I will do well in this country."

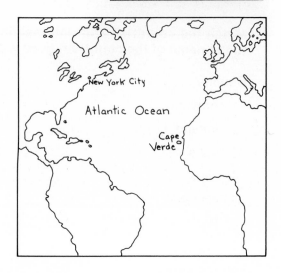

A. Complete the following sentences. Circle your answers.

1. João Mendes is
   a. Cape Verde.   b. Cape Verdean.   c. Africa.

2. Cape Verde is a country
   a. in the United States.   b. in Africa.   c. in the Atlantic Ocean.

3. João has a job as
   a. an accountant.   b. a cashier.   c. a college professor.

4. João is probably
   a. stupid.   b. hard-working.   c. cheap.

B. João wants to be an accountant because he likes taking care of money problems. Match the following likes or interests and careers. The first one is done for you.

Likes/Interests	Careers
_e_ 1. taking care of animals	a. author
_____ 2. playing sports for a salary	b. pharmacist
_____ 3. writing books	c. fashion designer
_____ 4. growing food and raising animals	d. reporter
_____ 5. mixing medicines and chemicals	e. veterinarian
_____ 6. writing stories for newspapers and television	f. farmer
_____ 7. drawing and creating new clothes and hats	g. professional athlete

Skill Objectives: Reading for details; making inferences; developing career vocabulary. Read the story aloud or have one or more volunteers read it. Review/introduce new vocabulary. Display a world map and have students find Cape Verde. If you have students from Cape Verde, have them tell about it. *Part A:* Do the first item orally with the class, then have them complete the others independently. *Part B:* Read over the instructions with the students and be sure they understand the connection between one's interests and one's possible occupational choices. Do item 1 orally; have students write *e* on the line. Then have them complete the page independently.

78

My Country and Yours: Writing a Description

Ireland is a small country in the North Atlantic. It is near England. Ireland is famous for many things. It is famous for its green countryside. In some parts of Ireland there are miles and miles of rolling, green fields. Other parts of Ireland are gray and rocky. Sometimes the weather in Ireland is chilly and damp. It rains a lot in Ireland; that's one reason the fields are so green.

Dublin is the capital of Ireland. Dublin is a beautiful old city. There are many small squares and parks in Dublin. O'Connell Street, in the center of Dublin, is very wide. There are fine stores on it. There is a very famous university in the city. It is called Trinity College.

The Irish people love to sing and dance and tell stories. I'm Irish; Ireland is my home. I think it's a wonderful country.

A. Answer each of the questions below. Use short answers. The first one is done for you.

1. Where is Ireland? _It's in the North Atlantic._____

2. What country is Ireland near? _____

3. What is the capital of Ireland? _____

4. What university is in Dublin? _____

5. What do the Irish love to do? _____

_____

B. Now write about your country. Use more paper if you need to.

_____

_____

_____

_____

_____

_____

_____

_____

_____

_____

Skill Objectives: Reading for details; writing an informative essay. Read the section aloud as students follow along, or have volunteers read it. Explain unfamiliar words. Have students reread the text silently. Discuss some or all of the comprehension questions, then assign the page as independent work. Students should use the text as a model as they write original essays about their native (or ancestral) countries. Allow time for students to read their essays aloud to the class.

Dear Dot

Dear Dot—

This is my problem. I want to be an actor, but my father says, "No!" I want to take drama classes next year. My father says, "Take computer programming." I don't want to go to college. My father says, "Go to college. Get an education." My father is not a college graduate, so it is important to him. But I want to act, not study. What can I do?

Hamlet

1. What does Hamlet want to be? _____

_____

2. What classes does he want to take? _____

_____

3. What does his father want him to take? _____

_____

4. Is his father a college graduate? _____

_____

5. What is your advice for Hamlet? Circle your answer.

   a. Do what your father says.   c. Take both classes if possible.

   b. Do what you want to do.   d. Leave home.

6. Now read Dot's answer. See if your answer is the same. If your answer is different, tell why you disagree. Dot's advice is below.

Dear Hamlet—

Listen to your father. Take computer programming and drama. Today you want to be an actor. Tomorrow you may want to be an accountant. Remember, most actors go to college nowadays. The more you know, the better off you are. Good luck.

Dot

Skill Objectives: Reading comprehension; making judgments. Have students recall the problems presented on previous "Dear Dot" pages. Read the letter aloud as students follow along, or have a volunteer read it. Explain unfamiliar words. Be sure the students understand why the boy has signed his letter, "Hamlet." Ask the students to reread the letter, then answer questions 1-5. Correct the first four answers, then let students compare their choice of advice. Read Dot's answer. Let students tell why they agree or disagree with Dot and offer other possible solutions.

There Is, There Are

A. Fill in the missing word. The first two are done for you.

1. There ___is___ one airport in Boston.

2. There ___are___ ten students in the class.

3. There _____ few cars in the parking lot.

4. There _____ a letter on the table for you.

5. There _____ many universities in Dallas.

6. There _____ a big park in this city.

B. Write the negative sentence. Then write the question. The first one is done for you.

1. There are three banks on Main Street.

   Negative: _There aren't any banks on Main Street._

   Question: _Are there any banks on Main Street?_

2. There are a few letters on the desk.

   Negative: _____

   Question: _____

3. There are two hospitals in Littleton.

   Negative: _____

   Question: _____

4. There are several students from Mexico in my class.

   Negative: _____

   Question: _____

C. Write the question that goes with each answer. The first one is done for you.

1. There are 15 hospitals in Fort Worth.

   Question: _How many hospitals are there in Fort Worth?_

2. There are 14 students from Vietnam in my school.

   Question: _____

3. There are more than seven million people in Los Angeles.

   Question: _____

Skill Objectives: *There is/are*; asking questions; making negative statements. Write on the board, *There is . . . There are . . . There aren't any . . . .* Have each student make at least one statement about the school, the classroom, or his/her desk using one of these sentence starters. Then ask a few "How many . . .?" questions. Let volunteers ask other "How many . . .?" questions. Go over the entire page as an oral group activity before assigning as independent written work.

Plurals: More than One

Learn and follow rules for spelling plurals.

Plural means more than one. **Read the rules for spelling plural words.**

RULE	SINGULAR	PLURAL
Add -s to most nouns.	book boy	books boys
Change -y nouns to -ies if -y follows a consonant.*	city	cities
Add -es to -ss, -sh, -ch, and -x nouns.	class dish watch box	classes dishes watches boxes

RULE	SINGULAR	PLURAL
Add -es to -o nouns if -o follows a consonant.*	potato tomato	potatoes tomatoes
Add -s to -o nouns if -o follows a vowel.**	radio	radios
Exceptions	child man woman foot mouse tooth	children men women feet mice teeth

*Consonants: b c d f g h j k l m n p q r s t v w x y

**Vowels: a e i o u

A. **Write the plural form of each word.** The first one is done for you.

1. egg _eggs_
2. shoe _____
3. country _____
4. church _____
5. bridge _____
6. hotel _____
7. blouse _____
8. chair _____
9. taxi _____
10. peach _____
11. doctor _____
12. suit _____
13. tooth _____
14. shirt _____
15. student _____
16. berry _____

17. name _____
18. man _____
19. daughter _____
20. banana _____
21. orange _____
22. baby _____
23. apple _____
24. nurse _____
25. jacket _____
26. lawyer _____
27. stool _____
28. woman _____
29. pilot _____
30. foot _____
31. child _____
32. bus _____

33. secretary _____
34. letter _____
35. friend _____
36. belt _____
37. book _____
38. library _____
39. radio _____
40. brother _____
41. brush _____
42. sandwich _____
43. dog _____
44. carrot _____
45. cemetery _____
46. rug _____
47. family _____
48. cousin _____

B. **Choose 25 of these words you know well. Write a sentence for each one. Underline the plurals you use in the sentence.** For example: "My <u>friends</u> are coming to town."

Skill Objectives: Learning spelling rules for forming plurals; writing original sentences. Read and discuss as necessary the rules in the box. *Part A*: Do the first ten examples as a group activity, reviewing the applicable rules and the pronunciations. Then assign the page as independent work. After students have completed Part B, ask each one to read his or her favorite sentence aloud.

82

What's Happening at School Today?

A. Read the sentences carefully. Then write the number of the sentence next to the picture it describes. The first one is done for you.

1. In one classroom, a girl is sharpening a pencil.

2. In the gym, students are exercising.

3. In the hall, a boy is opening his locker.

4. In one classroom, two girls are whispering.

5. In the home economics class, students are cooking.

6. In the cafeteria, two boys are fighting.

7. In one classroom, a boy is goofing off.

8. In the hall, a boy is getting a drink.

B. On your own paper, write about the picture. You may use the sentences above or make up sentences of your own. Start with the following title and topic sentence.

One Day at Park Junior High

It's a busy day at Park Junior High School.

D A T A   B A N K

cooking	getting a drink	sharpening a pencil	exercising
fighting	goofing off	opening his locker	whispering

Skill Objectives: Present progressive; writing a paragraph. Teach/review the words and phrases in the Data Bank. Ask volunteers to pantomime specific actions. Ask, "What is/are (he/she/they) doing?" Reinforce as many phrases as possible this way. Have students search the picture to answer two questions about each Data Bank word or phrase: "Who is (cooking)?" "Where is/are (he/she/they) (cooking)?" Teach necessary vocabulary (home economics class, etc.). Students may read the sentences aloud, then complete the page independently.

Interviewing:
This School

A. **Interview your teachers, the school secretary, or the assistant principal to find out the answers to these questions.**

1. How many students are there in this school? _____

2. How many students are there from Mexico? _____

3. How many classrooms are there? _____

4. How many teachers are there? _____

5. How many librarians are there? _____

6. How many guidance counselors are there? _____

7. How many buses are there? _____

8. Are there any TVs in the school? _____

9. Are there any computers? _____

10. Are there any students from Vietnam? _____

B. **Now write a paragraph about your school.**

Here are some interesting facts about my school.

_____

_____

_____

_____

_____

_____

_____

_____

_____

_____

84

Skill Objectives: *There is/are;* **interviewing; writing a paragraph.** If possible, ask the principal, assistant principal, or school secretary to visit your class armed with the necessary statistics. If this is not possible, research these questions yourself, and let the class interview you. Have students use the information to make oral statements about their school. Example: "There are . . . students in this school." Then assign Part B as independent written work. Students may refer to the sample paragraph on page 127 for format if they need to.

Reading a Chart

The following chart shows the nationality and the first language of students at Central School. **Read the chart and look at the box under it.**

Nationality	First Language	Number of Students
American	English	324
Mexican	Spanish	101
Guatemalan	Spanish	56
Puerto Rican	Spanish	34
Vietnamese	Vietnamese	21
Haitian	French	12
Lebanese	Arabic	4
Korean	Korean	3
Japanese	Japanese	1

There is . . . (used when talking about one thing or person)
There are . . . (used when talking about more than one thing or person)
There are a few. (used when talking about a small number)
There are many. (used when talking about a large number)

A. Answer these questions. Use complete sentences. The first one is done for you.

1. How many Americans are there in this school? *There are 324 Americans.*

2. How many Haitians are there? _____

3. How many Spanish speakers are there? _____

   _____

4. How many Vietnamese are there? _____

5. How many Japanese are there? _____

6. How many students are there all together? _____

   _____

B. Now answer these questions. The first two are done for you.

1. Are there any students from Korea? *Yes, there are a few.*

2. Are there any students from China? *No, there aren't any.*

3. Are there any students from Mexico? _____

4. Are there any students from Lebanon? _____

5. Are there any students from Spain? _____

6. Are there any Americans? _____

Skill Objectives: *There is/are;* **finding information from a chart.** Have students read the data on the chart aloud. Read the box under the chart with the students and make sure all understand both concepts: when to use "there is" and when to use "there are," and when to use "there are few" and when to use "there are many." Go through all the items in Parts A and B orally before assigning the page as independent written work.

85

Reading a Circle Chart

Circle charts are often used to show percents. This circle chart shows the first language of students at the El Rancho School. Use the chart to answer the questions.

EL RANCHO SCHOOL
First Language of Students

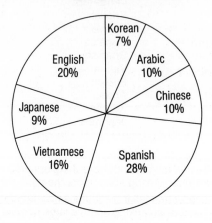

A. Answer these questions. The first one is done for you.

1. What percent (%) of the students have Japanese as their first language? __*9%*__

2. What percent have Korean as their first language? _____

3. What percent have Vietnamese as their first language? _____

4. What percent come from families whose first language is not English? _____

B. Read these statements and put a *T* in the blank if the statement is true, an *F* if the statement is false, and a *?* if the chart doesn't give you the information. The first two are done for you.

1. __*T*__ There are more Spanish speakers at this school than any other group.

2. __*?*__ Most of the Spanish speakers are from Mexico.

3. _____ There are more Chinese-speaking students than Japanese-speaking students.

4. _____ There are as many Arabic speakers as there are Korean speakers.

5. _____ Only a few of the Chinese speakers are from Hong Kong.

6. _____ There are more students whose first language is Vietnamese than there are whose first language is English.

7. _____ There are more whose first language is English than any other group.

8. _____ 42% of the students are from Asian countries (Korea, Japan, Vietnam, and China.)

C. Circle charts are sometimes called pie charts. **On another sheet of paper, write one or more sentences telling why this name is used.**

Skill Objectives: Interpreting a circle chart; answering true-false questions; making inferences. Read the directions aloud to the students. Review the meaning of "percent." Have students read the title above the circle chart; be sure they understand what is meant by "first language." Review the concepts of "more than" and "as many as." Work through all the questions in Parts A and B before assigning the page as independent work.

86

Quincy Market:
Reading for Details

In the city of Boston there are many universities, many students, many people from many different countries, and many good restaurants. In one building in Boston there are four American restaurants, two Italian restaurants, one Greek restaurant, and one Arabic restaurant. This building is called Quincy Market. The building is 150 years old. It is old on the outside, but it is new on the inside.

Quincy Market is part of a big shopping center. All the buildings are old, but there are modern stores in them. There are shoe stores, clothing stores, stores for jewelry, candy, and toys, and many other kinds of stores. Outside, there are places for people to sit and rest and watch the people.

Nearby there is an outdoor market, where you can buy fruit and vegetables. There are fresh red tomatoes, orange carrots, and green cucumbers in the vegetable stands. In the fruit stands there are bananas, apples, oranges, peaches, and plums. There are also butcher shops, cheese shops, and fish shops. You can buy chicken and turkey and duck, beef and lamb and pork, and all kinds of fish and shellfish. Everyone is shouting, trying to get you to buy the things he or she is selling. There is a big difference between an outdoor market and a supermarket!

Quincy Market is a fun place to go! If you like to eat, don't miss it when you go to Boston.

Read each sentence below. Write *T* if the sentence is true. Write *F* if the sentence is false. Write *?* if the answer is impossible to know.

__*T*__ 1. Boston is a mixture of many different people and cultures.

__*?*__ 2. The outdoor market is more popular than the indoor market.

_____ 3. There are only a few restaurants in the Quincy market area.

_____ 4. The buildings are old and so are the shops inside them.

_____ 5. There are eight different restaurants in one building.

_____ 6. All of the restaurants are cheap.

_____ 7. You can sit outdoors in the Quincy Market area.

_____ 8. You can buy fresh fruits and vegetables in the indoor market.

_____ 9. The outdoor market can sometimes be noisy.

_____ 10. Quincy Market is usually crowded.

_____ 11. An outdoor market is the same as a supermarket.

_____ 12. An outdoor market is expensive.

_____ 13. There are tomatoes and cucumbers in the fruit stands.

_____ 14. It's fun to go to Quincy Market.

Skill Objective: Reading for details. Read the selection aloud as students follow along (Quincy in Massachusetts is pronounced KWIN-zee, with a *z* sound). Explain unfamiliar vocabulary. Have students locate Boston on a U.S. map. Then write these sentences on the board: *Boston is a city in Massachusetts. Quincy Market is in New York City. Quincy Market is expensive.* Have the class decide which statement is true, which is false, and which is impossible to know from reading the story. Ask students to reread the story silently before completing the page independently.

Chicago: Facts and Opinions

Mr. Peters is in a taxi. He is coming from O'Hare airport in Chicago. He is going to the North Side of the city. His taxi driver is talking to him.

"Chicago is a great town. I love it. We have two baseball teams here, the Cubs and the White Sox. I like the Cubs. The White Sox are boring and they're losers, too. I never go to their games. But there's a lot more to Chicago than baseball. Look around. We're in the city now. This is Michigan Avenue. There's the John Hancock Center. That building is 100 stories high! That's too high, if you ask me. If there is a fire on the 85th or 90th floor, how are the firemen going to put it out? There's no chance. . . . Look over there. There's a larger build-ing. It's the Sears Tower. That building is 110 stories high! . . . Do you see those round buildings? Those are the Marina City apartments. Those buildings have 60 floors each. Thousands of people live in each one. Imagine that, all those people in two buildings. It's terrible to have so many neighbors. . . . There's the Merchandise Mart. That's another big building. Do you know what's in that building? There are stores, restaurants, a bank, a post office, a radio station and a T.V. station. It's great, but don't ever go there on a Saturday! It's too crowded. . . . Well, here we are. There's plenty more to see in this city. Remember, ask any cab driver about Chicago. We know everything about this town!"

The taxi driver is giving Mr. Peters lots of information. Many things the driver says are FACTS. *Facts are true statements that you can read or check in an encyclopedia or other reference book.* Other things the driver says are OPINIONS. *Opinions are what a person thinks about something.* They are true for the person saying them, but they are not true for everyone. You cannot check them in a reference book. Two people can have completely different OPINIONS about the same FACTS.

Look at each sentence below. If it is a FACT, write FACT next to it. If it is an OPINION, write OPINION next to it.

1. Chicago has two baseball teams. _____

2. The White Sox are a boring team. _____

3. The John Hancock Center is on Michigan Avenue. _____

4. The John Hancock Center is too tall. _____

5. The Sears Tower is 110 stories high. _____

6. Thousands of people live in Marina City Apartments. _____

7. It's terrible to have thousands of neighbors. _____

8. There are many stores and restaurants in the Merchandise Mart. _____

9. The Merchandise Mart is too crowded on Saturday. _____

10. Taxi drivers know all about Chicago. _____

Skill Objective: Distinguishing between fact and opinion. Read the story aloud as students follow along. Have students locate Chicago on a U.S. map. Read the explanation of the difference between a fact and an opinion. Write the following sentences on the board: *Chicago is the largest city in Illinois. Chicago is a great town.* Let students decide which is a fact and which is an opinion, then explain their reasons. Have students reread the story before completing the Fact vs. Opinion exercise. Let students compare and discuss answers.

Dallas:
The Main Idea

Dallas is a big city in Texas. Dallas is about 1400 miles from New York and about 1300 miles from San Francisco. It is nearly 300 miles from Galveston, but only 28 miles from Fort Worth.

There are many streets in Dallas. There are hundreds of tall buildings, short buildings, old buildings, and new buildings. You can see all of Dallas from one very tall building.

Two small towns are in the middle of Dallas! The towns are University Park and Highland Park. The Trinity River is in the middle of Dallas, too.

There are more than 200 schools and 16 libraries in Dallas. There are 25 radio stations and 11 TV stations. There are more than 100 banks, and hundreds of churches. There are well known stores, big museums, busy theaters, and fine restaurants. And there are over a million people in the city, and many more in the suburbs.

Dallas is a very big city! There is lots of traffic and noise. But people like the big stores and restaurants. They like the theaters and the museums. And they love to watch the football games with the Dallas Cowboys!

How about you? How do you like "Big D?"

A. What is the main idea of this story? Circle the right answer.

a. Dallas is far away from New York and San Francisco.

b. There is lots of traffic and noise in Dallas.

c. Dallas is a big, busy city.

d. There are many schools, libraries, and radio and TV stations in Dallas.

B. Write questions to go with the answers.

1. _____? About 1300 miles.

2. _____? It is in the middle of Dallas.

3. _____? There are more than 200.

4. _____? There are nearly a million.

5. _____? They are a football team.

6. _____? It's a name for Dallas.

C. Write a name for the story.

_____

D. Now copy the story about Dallas on another piece of paper. Use your best handwriting. Put your name for the story at the top.

Skill Objectives: Identifying main idea; making inferences; forming questions. Read the selection aloud. Explain any new words. Have students locate the cities mentioned in the first paragraph on a map. Write on the board, *How many . . .? How far . . .? What . . .? Where . . .?* Have students use these forms to ask questions about the selection. *Part A:* Have students compare their answers and discuss why only one choice states the main idea. If you wish, do Parts B and C as group activities before assigning as written work. *Part D:* This is the first opportunity in this book for students to handwrite a multi-paragraph selection. Check for accuracy.

Using a Pay Telephone

A. **Write the missing word.** The first one is done for you.

1. The woman is _____*entering*_____ the phone booth.

2. She is _____ a number in the phone book.

3. She is _____ the number.

4. She is _____ the phone.

5. She is _____ a coin or coins.

6. She is _____ the number.

7. She is _____ to someone.

8. She is _____ the phone.

D A T A   B A N K

talking	dialing	hanging up	picking up
looking for	writing down	depositing	entering

B. When do you use the telephone? **On another sheet of paper write the heading,**

I use the telephone when I am . . .

Write as many endings to the sentence as you can. Use the *-ing* form of verbs. Some possible answers are:

. . . going away and need information about schedules.
. . . making a dentist's appointment.
. . . calling a friend.

Skill Objectives: Following and naming a sequence; using present progressive. Teach/review the vocabulary in the Data Bank. Have a student read one word or phrase. A second student will say the number of the matching picture. A third student will put the word(s) into a complete sentence. Example: "Talking." "Number 7." "She is talking (on the phone/to someone)." Repeat this activity for all eight phrases. Provide vocabulary help as needed. *Part B*: Be sure students understand the directions. Discuss if necessary before assigning the page for independent work.

Dear Dot

Dear Dot—

I am Vietnamese. There are no other Vietnamese kids in my school. I don't fit in here. I still don't speak English very well, and I feel stupid when I make mistakes. There are some girls I want to know, but I am too shy to talk to them. I am not happy, and I miss my country. What can I do?

Homesick and Sad

1. Where is the student from? _____

2. How many Vietnamese students are there in her school? _____

3. What language is she learning? _____

4. When does she feel stupid? _____

_____

5. Who does she want to know? _____

_____

6. What is your advice for Homesick and Sad? Circle your answer.

   a. Learn more English and make more friends.   c. Get a job.

   b. Go back to your own country.   d. Read more and watch television.

7. Now read Dot's answer. See if your answer is the same. If your answer is different, tell why you disagree. Dot's advice is below.

Dear Homesick and Sad—

Join a club or another kind of extra-curricular activity. Invite the girls you want to know to your house. Don't be so shy—ask them to help you practice your English. Teach them some words in Vietnamese. Then they will understand how hard English can be for you. Don't be afraid to ask for more help from other students and your teachers. Most people are happy to help if they know what your problem is.

Dot

Skill Objectives: Reading comprehension; making judgments. Read the letter aloud or have a volunteer read it as students follow along. Explain any unfamiliar words. Ask students to reread the letter silently, then answer questions 1-6. Correct the first five answers, then let students compare their choice of advice. Read Dot's answer together. Let students tell why they agree or disagree with Dot's solution and perhaps offer some different suggestions of their own.

91

Watch the Clock

What time is it? Write the sentence. The first one is done for you.

1. *It's twenty to three.*

2. _____

3. _____

4. _____

5. _____

6. _____

7. _____

8. _____

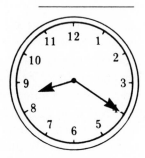

9. _____

10. _____

11. _____

12. _____

14. _____

15. _____

16. _____

13. _____

Skill Objective: Telling time to the nearest five minutes. Go over this page as an oral group activity. Name a clock by its number and ask a student to tell the time. Give all students a chance to respond at least once to the question, "What time is it?" For further practice, state a time and have the students identify, by number, the correct clock. After sufficient oral practice, assign the page for independent written work.

92

Time Zones

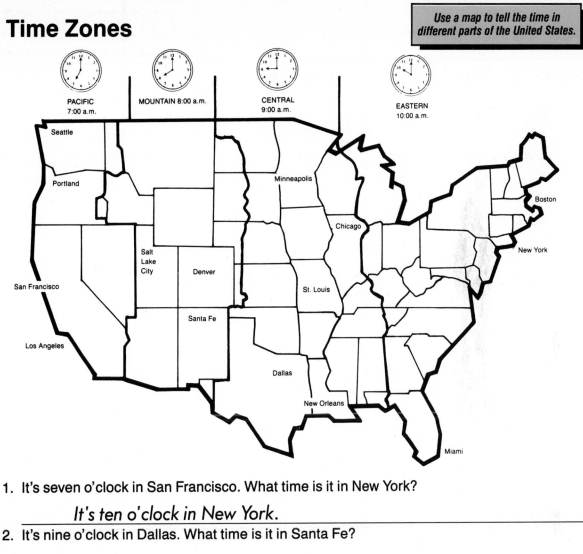

1. It's seven o'clock in San Francisco. What time is it in New York?

   It's ten o'clock in New York.

2. It's nine o'clock in Dallas. What time is it in Santa Fe?

3. It's ten o'clock in Miami. What time is it in Denver?

4. It's eight o'clock in Denver. What time is it in Salt Lake City?

5. If it is noon in Boston, what time is it in Los Angeles?

6. If it is noon in Chicago, what time is it in Seattle?

7. If it is noon in Minneapolis, what time is it in New Orleans?

8. If it is one p.m. in St. Louis, what time is it in Boston?

Skill Objectives: Interpreting a map; computing time zone differences. Study the map with the class. If applicable, have students locate and plot their city or town on the map. Point out the four time zones. (Explain that there are additional time zones for eastern Canada, Alaska, and Hawaii.) Using the map, ask, for each city, "What time is it in . . .?" Next, write the actual time on the board (rounded to the nearest hour). Say, "It's . . . o'clock here. What time is it in . . .?" When the class shows understanding of the concept, assign the page for independent written work.

Where Are They Going?

Where's Peter going?		He's going to the bus station.
Why?		He's going to meet a friend.
When is he coming back?		He's coming back at 9:00.

A. Look at the picture. Answer the questions.

1. Where's he going? _____

2. Why? _____

3. When is he coming back? _____

4. Where are they going? _____

5. Why? _____

6. When are they coming back? _____

7. Where's she going? _____

8. Why? _____

9. When is she coming back? _____

B. On another paper, write sentences from this chart.

Example: Lisa is going to the library this afternoon.
             She's going to return a book.

	WHO	WHERE	WHEN	WHY
1.	Lisa	library	this afternoon	return a book
2.	Rob	music store	tonight	buy a cassette
3.	I	cafeteria	now	have lunch
4.	You	airport	tomorrow	take a trip

Skill Objectives: Using present progressive as future; using *going to* future; making inferences. Study the example box with the class. Be sure students understand how to use information in the picture clues. Work through Part A as an oral group activity. Answers to "Why?" should vary and provide a springboard for discussion about the different reasons people go to different places. *Part B:* Be sure students understand the instructions for Part B. Go over the example, showing how each part of each sentence comes directly from the chart. Then assign the page as independent written work.

Pronouns

A. Finish these conversations. Fill in the missing words.

1. Whose umbrella is this?
   Give it to _____, please.
   It's Jim's.

2. Whose shoes are these?
   Give them to _____, please.
   They're Judy's.

3. Whose papers are these?
   They're our papers.
   Please give _____ to _____.

4. Is this your pencil?
   Yes, please give _____ to _____.

B. Write the missing pronoun. The first one is done for you.

1. Mary's tired so her sister is helping ___*her*___.   (she, her)

2. Baby Bill is hungry so his mother is feeding _____.   (he, him)

3. Tom and Mary are sick so I'm helping _____.   (they, them)

4. I'm busy at work so my secretary is helping _____.   (me, I)

5. You are tired so we are helping _____.   (us, you)

6. We are busy so our friends are helping _____.   (us, we)

7. My dog is hungry so I'm feeding _____.   (it's, it)

8. My clothes are dirty so I'm washing _____.   (they, them)

9. Our stove is dirty so my brother is cleaning _____.   (them, it)

10. My car is broken so I'm fixing _____.   (its, it)

Skill Objective: Using pronouns and possessives. Write these sentences on the board: *Give the book to Ann. Give the money to Jim and Ed. Give the cards to Maria and me.* Underline the direct object. Have a student repeat each sentence using the pronoun replacement. ("Give *it* to Ann.") Underline the indirect object. Have a student substitute both pronouns. ("Give *it* to *her*.") Then ask, "Whose book is it?" ("It's Ann's.") Have students read and complete Part A orally. Do some or all of Part B orally before assigning the pages as written work.

Going Places

Read each paragraph carefully. Where are the people going? Write the name of the place.

1. Many people are going here this morning. They are going to deposit money, cash checks, and pay bills. Where are these people going?

   _____

2. Other people are going here. They are going to sit in the sun, swim, and dive. Where are they going?

   _____

3. At this place people are going to go to class, to the library, to meet their friends, and to study. Where are they going?

   _____

4. At this place, people are going to read, take out and return books, and do homework. Where are they going?

   _____

5. Some people are going here to pick up packages. Others are going to mail letters and to buy stamps. Where are all these people going?

   _____

6. At this place people are going to buy drinks and candy, eat popcorn, and sit in the dark. Where are they going?

   _____

7. Many people are going here today. Some are going to buy meat and cheese. Others are buying milk and vegetables. Where are these people going?

   _____

8. At this place, people are going to buy flowers, visit sick friends, get X-rays and prescriptions. Where are they going?

   _____

9. Some people are going here to meet friends. Other people are going on vacations. They are all going to see many large planes. Where are these people going?

   _____

10. People are going here in their cars. They are going to buy gasoline and fill their tires with air. Some of them will talk to mechanics about their cars. Where are these people going?

   _____

D A T A   B A N K

airport	beach	grocery store	library	post office
bank	gas station	hospital	movie theater	school

Skill Objectives: Understanding uses of *going, going to*; drawing conclusions. Teach/review the vocabulary in the Data Bank. For each place, ask, "What do people do at/in a(n) . . .?" Do the first one or two examples as a group exercise, then assign as independent written work.

A Trip to the "Big Apple"

Tom is going to the airport at 10:00. He's taking his suitcase and his ticket. Tom is taking a vacation in New York City. His mother is going with him. They are going to stay in a nice hotel in Manhattan.

The first thing they are going to do in New York is visit the World Trade Center. The World Trade Center is the tallest building in New York City. Tom and his mother are going to eat lunch in the restaurant on the top floor.

What else are they going to do? They're going to take the bus to the Metropolitan Museum and then the subway to the Empire State Building. They're going to ride the ferry to the Statue of Liberty. Tom is going to climb all 168 steps to the top! Tom and his mother are going to have a good time in "the Big Apple."

A. What is this story mostly about? Circle the answer.

a. Tom's mother

b. Airplanes and airports

c. A vacation in New York City

d. Visting the World Trade Center

B. Answer these questions.

1. How are Tom and his mother traveling to New York? _____

_____

2. Where are they going to sleep while they're in New York? _____

_____

3. What is "the Big Apple?" _____

_____

C. Write the questions. Then practice asking and answering with a classmate.

1. _____ He's going to the airport.

2. _____ His mother is.

3. _____ The World Trade Center is.

4. _____ They're going to ride the ferry.

5. _____ There are 168.

Skill Objectives: Identifying main idea; making inferences; asking questions. Read the text aloud as students follow along, or have a volunteer read it. Explain any new vocabulary. Have students reread the selection silently before answering the questions. Depending on the skill level of your group, you may wish to discuss the questions as a group before assigning as independent work. If students work independently, be sure to discuss and compare answers after completion.

97

A Field Trip

Mr. Beck is a history teacher in Rapid City, South Dakota. South Dakota is a state in the Midwest. Tomorrow, he and his class are going on a field trip. They are going to the Black Hills, the mountains of South Dakota. They are going to see the faces of four American Presidents: George Washington, Thomas Jefferson, Abraham Lincoln, and Theodore Roosevelt. They are not going to see the Presidents themselves, but they are not going to see pictures or photographs of the Presidents either. They are going to see the Presidents' faces in the mountains!

An artist named Gutzon Borglum carved the stone faces. They are 60 feet high and are a part of Mount Rushmore, a mountain in the Black Hills. The faces are so big that you can see them 60 miles away. Mr. Beck's students are going to take pictures and write stories about their visit. If you ever travel across the country, make sure you visit this famous monument.

A. Answer the following questions. Use short answers. The first one is done for you.

1. Where is South Dakota? _____*in the Midwest*_____

2. What is Mr. Beck's class going to do tomorrow? _____

3. Where is the class going? _____

4. What are they going to see? _____

5. What did Gutzon Borglum do? _____

6. How big are the faces? _____

7. What are Mr. Beck's students going to do on the trip? _____

   _____

8. At what distance can you see the faces of the Presidents? _____

B. What is this story mostly about? Circle the best answer.

a. the Presidents   c. Mount Rushmore

b. Mr. Beck's class   d. North Dakota

Skill Objective: Identifying main idea and details. Read the selection aloud or have a volunteer read it. Explain unfamiliar words. Display a map of the United States. Help students locate the Midwest, South Dakota, and, if possible, the Black Hills, Mount Rushmore, and Rapid City. Ask students to reread the selection silently before independently completing the page. Correct the students' answers together. Have students discuss their answer choice in Part B and explain why only answer c expresses the main idea of the story.

98

Dear Dot

Dear Dot—

My problem is this. I like a girl in my class, but she doesn't know I exist. She is very popular. She is always going to a party or the movies or the arcade with her girlfriends. I'm going to ask her out, but I'm very nervous. I don't know what to say or how to act. And what if she says no? I'm afraid of looking stupid.

Silent Admirer

1. Is the girl in the boy's class? _____

2. Is she popular? _____

3. What is he going to do? _____

4. What is he afraid of? _____

5. What is your advice for Silent Admirer? Circle your answer.
   a. Send her a letter.
   b. Ask one of her friends if she likes you.
   c. Be confident; don't worry about her answer.
   d. Forget about her; ask a different girl.

6. Now play the part of Dear Dot and write your answer to Silent Admirer.

   Dear Silent Admirer _____ ,

   _____

   _____

   _____

   _____

   _____

   _____

   _____

Skill Objectives: Reading comprehension; making judgments; writing a letter. Read the letter aloud as students follow along, or have a volunteer read it. Explain any unfamiliar words. Ask students to reread the letter silently and answer questions 1-5. Correct the first four answers, then let students compare their choice of advice. Finally. have students assume Dot's role and write a response in their own words. Help them with letter format if necessary.

99

What Do You Have to Do?

Use what you already know to tell what people have to do.

A. Bill has some problems. Write what he *has* to do to solve his problems. The first one is done for you.

1. Bill's room is messy. _He has to clean his room._

2. The dishes are dirty. _____

3. His clothes are on the bed. _____

4. Juan is thirsty. _____

5. The waste baskets are full. _____

6. It's time for dinner. _____

7. The rugs are dirty. _____

8. The dog is hungry. _____

D A T A   B A N K   A

feed the dog	**drink some water**	**wash the dishes**	**hang up his clothes**
set the table	**empty the waste baskets**	**vacuum the rugs**	**clean his room**

B. Here are some more problems. Write what the people *have* to do to solve the problems. The first one is done for you.

Problems *Solutions*

1. They have an English test tomorrow. _They have to study._

2. My bike is broken. _____

3. Susan is very sick. _____

4. My father's birthday is tomorrow. _____

5. There is no milk in my refrigerator. _____

6. John is coming to a red light. _____

7. They are going to Paris soon. _____

8. Our car is out of gas. _____

D A T A   B A N K   B

call the doctor	**buy some milk**	**buy a present**	**stop the car**
get passports	**go to a gas station**	**study**	**fix my bike**

Skill Objectives: Using *have to, has to*; drawing conclusions. *Part A:* Teach/review the phrases in Data Bank A. Have a volunteer mime one of the actions. Ask the class, "What does (Luis) have to do?" ("He has to set the table.") Repeat for all eight expressions. Read the directions. Do one or two examples with the class, then have students work independently. *Part B:* Teach/review vocabulary in Data Bank B. Do the exercise orally before assigning as independent work. Listen for use of the correct pronoun and verb form.

Can and Can't

A. Read the question and look at the picture. Then answer the question. The first one is done for you.

1. What sport can he play?

He can play soccer.

_____

2. What instrument can she play?

_____

_____

3. What game can they play?

_____

_____

4. What sport can you play?

_____

_____

5. What instrument can they play?

_____

_____

B. Now write a story about yourself. What can you do? What can't you do? Use more paper if you need to.

_____

_____

_____

_____

_____

_____

_____

_____

_____

Skill Objectives: Using modals *can*, *can't*; writing a story. *Part A*: Do this section as an oral group activity before assigning as written work. *Part B*: Write the following questions on the board: *What sports can you play? What games can you play? What instruments can you play? What languages can you speak? Can you ride a bike? Can you type? Can you make coffee?* Have students suggest other *Can you . . .?* questions, then discuss what they can and can't do. Encourage students to read their finished stories aloud.

Interviewing: Can You?

Interview two classmates. Write their names above the two columns. Then write their answers in the box. Report your findings to the class.

THINGS PEOPLE DO	Name: STUDENT 1	STUDENT 2
1. Can you skate?		
2. Can you play the guitar?		
3. Can you dance?		
4. Can you play Ping-Pong?		
5. Can you run a mile?		
6. Can you speak Spanish?		
7. Can you play chess?		
8. Can you swim?		
9. Can you cook?		
10. Can you play the drums?		
11. Can you ski?		
12. Can you play soccer?		
13. Can you type?		
14. Can you drive?		
15. Can you ride a horse?		
16. Can you fix a car?		

Skill Objectives: Using modals *can, can't*; interviewing; using a chart. Teach/review the vocabulary on the page, then divide the class into groups of four. Each students should interview two other students from his/her group.

A Bike Trip

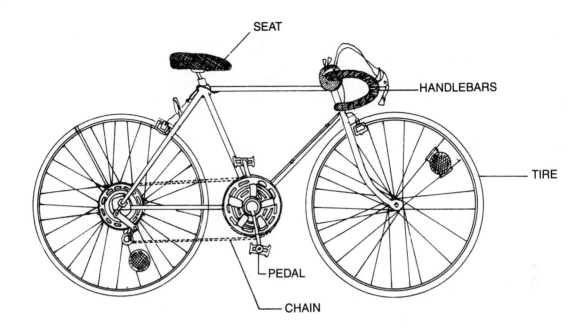

It's early in the morning and Peter is at the gas station. He's getting his bicycle ready for a long trip. He's polishing the handlebars. He's putting fresh grease on the chain. He's filling the tires with air. He's tightening the seat. Now he's ready to go.

This is Peter's first trip of the summer. He's a good rider. He's going to Crystal Lake. Crystal Lake is thirty miles away from Peter's house. Peter and his friends are riding to the lake together. They are going to stay there all day. At 6:00 they are going to ride home.

Answer these questions. The first one is done for you.

1. Where is Peter early in the morning? _He is at the gas station._

2. What is he doing to the handlebars of his bike? _____

3. What is he doing to the chain? _____

4. What is he doing to the tires? _____

5. What is he doing to the seat? _____

6. Where is Peter going? _____

7. Where is Crystal Lake? _____

8. Who is going with Peter? _____

9. When is Peter coming home? _____

Skill Objectives: Interpreting a diagram; reading for details. Study the bicycle diagram with the class. Go over the labeled parts. Read the story aloud as students follow along, or have a volunteer read it. Explain any unfamiliar words. (Point out that "bike" is another word for bicycle.) Ask the students to reread the story silently before answering the nine questions independently.

103

Jack's Car

Jack is going to drive to the rock concert. This is his car.

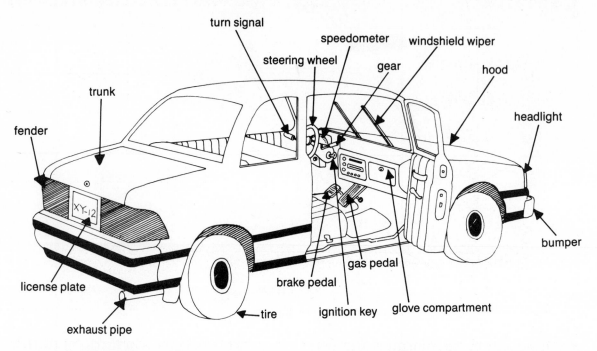

A. In the column at the right are some parts of Jack's car. Decide what each part does. Read the sentences on the left. Draw a line from the sentence to the part of the car that Jack will use. The first one is done for you.

1. It is raining.
2. It is getting dark.
3. It says 50 MPH.
4. Jack is stopping at a light.
5. Jack is shifting.
6. Jack is starting his car.
7. Jack is accelerating.

a. speedometer
b. brake pedal
c. windshield wipers
d. headlights
e. gas pedal
f. ignition key
g. gear

B. Now write about your car. If you don't have a car, write about your dream car. Tell as much as you can about it. What kind is it? What color is it? Is it old or new? How big is it? Use more paper if you need to.

_____

_____

_____

_____

_____

Skill Objectives: Interpreting a diagram; making inferences; writing a paragraph. Study the car diagram with the class. Ask questions about the labeled parts: "When do you use the windshield wipers/the headlights? How do you start/stop a car? When do the tail lights go on?" etc. *Part A:* Teach any new vocabulary, then assign for independent work. *Part B:* If possible, display magazine pictures of cars. If they wish, students may choose one of these pictures to describe.

Road Signs

Use words from the Data Bank to tell what the signs mean. The first one is done for you.

1.

   one way

2.

3.

4.

5.

6.

7.

8.

9.

10.

11.

12.

DATA BANK

hospital	airport ahead	railroad crossing
intersection	phone ahead	school zone
no left turn	food ahead	slippery when wet
no parking	one way	two way traffic

Skill Objective: Interpreting road signs. Teach/review the vocabulary on this page. Let students independently write the correct term under each road sign. Correct and discuss the answers as a class.

More Road Signs

Circle the traffic rule that goes with each sign. The first one is done for you.

a. You have to stop.
b. You can stop.
c. You can't stop.

a. You can't turn left.
b. You have to turn left.
c. You can turn left.

a. You can't turn right.
b. You have to turn right.
c. You can turn right.

a. You have to slip in the rain.
b. Careful! You can slip in the rain.
c. This road is always wet.

SPEED LIMIT 55

a. You can drive more than 55 mph.
b. You have to drive more than 55 mph.
c. You can't drive more than 55 mph.

FUEL AHEAD

a. You can get gas ahead.
b. You can't get gas ahead.
c. You have to get gas ahead.

a. You can drive both ways on this street.
b. You can only drive one way on this street.
c. You have to drive both ways on this street.

DO NOT PASS

a. You can pass other cars.
b. You have to pass other cars.
c. You have to stay behind other cars.

a. You have to watch for children.
b. You have to cross the street.
c. You can drive quickly.

a. You can park here.
b. You can't park here.
c. You have to park here.

Skill Objectives: Interpreting road signs; understanding modals *have to, can, can't*. Do the first one or two items as a group exercise. Be sure students understand the difference between *can* and *have to*. Emphasize the need to read each sentence carefully. Assign the page for independent work. Correct and discuss the answers together.

Dear Dot

Read a letter and write
an answer to it.

Dear Dot—

This is my problem. Ernesto, my brother, is good at everything. He can sing and dance and play the drums, and can speak <u>three</u> languages. Our friends call him "Ernesto the Great" or "Ernesto the Champ." I can write good stories, and I can play the guitar. How can I get people to pay attention to the things I am good at?

Little Brother Juan

1. What is Juan's problem? _____

_____

2. Name three things Ernesto can do. _____

_____

3. What can Juan do? _____

_____

4. Now write a letter to Little Brother Juan. Give him your advice. Tell him exactly what to do and what NOT to do.

Dear Juan _____ ,

_____

_____

_____

_____

_____

_____

_____

_____

Skill Objectives: Reading comprehension; making judgments; writing a letter. Read the letter aloud as students follow along, or have a
volunteer read it. Explain any unfamiliar words. Ask students to reread the letter silently, then answer questions 1-3. Correct their answers. Discuss
possible answers to question 4 and then have students write their solutions.

107

Parts of the Body

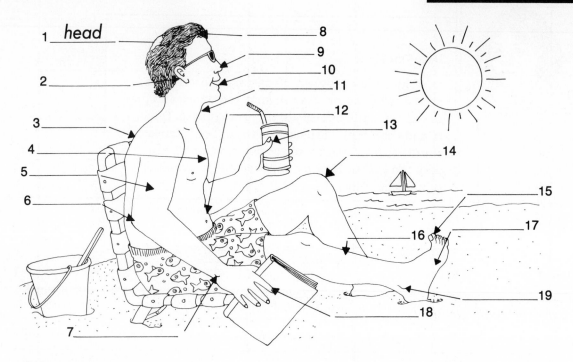

1. head

2. _____
3. _____
4. _____
5. _____
6. _____
7. _____

8. _____
9. _____
10. _____
11. _____
12. _____
13. _____
14. _____
15. _____
16. _____
17. _____
18. _____
19. _____

A. Write the name of each body part on the line. Use the words in Data Bank A. The first one is done for you.

DATA BANK A

ankle	chest	finger	head	mouth	throat	wrist
arm	ear	foot	knee	nose	thumb	
back	elbow	hair	leg	stomach	toe	

B. Use the words in Data Bank B to write a sentence about each person's problem.

1. *She has a headache.*   2. _____   3. _____

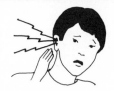 

4. _____   5. _____   6. _____

DATA BANK B

stomachache	sore throat	earache	backache	headache	broken leg

Skill Objectives: Building vocabulary; labeling a diagram; discussing ailments. Teach/review names of body parts. Play a reinforcement game: Point at various parts of your body and say, "This is my (ear). This is my (foot)." Students will touch that part of their bodies and repeat after you. Occasionally name a part incorrectly (point at your knee and say, "This is my ankle.") Students should correct you: "No! *This* is my knee." Keep the pace lively. Have students read aloud as a group the words in Data Bank A. Teach the new words in Part B and practice pronunciation before assigning the page as written work.

A Visit to the Doctor

A. Put the story in chronological order. The pictures and the numbers correspond. Use your dictionary if you have to.

_____ First, the doctor examines Amy's ears, nose and throat.

_____ Then the nurse weighs Amy. She's 121 pounds!

_____ Next, the doctor checks her back.

___1___ Every year, Amy goes to the doctor for a regular check-up.

_____ Before she leaves, Amy thanks Dr. Baker, shakes her hand and says goodbye.

_____ When Amy arrives, she sits in the waiting room and reads a magazine.

_____ Next, the nurse takes her blood pressure. It's normal.

_____ Then the nurse calls her into the examining room.

_____ The doctor also checks her heart, lungs, and stomach.

_____ In this room, Amy takes off her clothes and puts on a hospital gown.

_____ Then the nurse takes a blood sample to do some tests.

_____ After that, Dr. Baker comes in and says hello.

B. Now write the story in paragraph form. Use another piece of paper.

Skill Objectives: Sequencing events; using health-related vocabulary. On the board write, _checks, weighs, examines,_ and any other unfamiliar words from the page. Have students cover the bottom of the page and look only at the picture sequence. Introduce the patient as "Amy." Ask students to tell you about each picture. Start by asking, "What does Amy do first?" Encourage use of the simple present tense; point to the words on the board when appropriate. After all the pictures have been discussed, explain the instructions for Part A. Point out that the number _1_ has already been filled in. _Part B:_ Have students write the story in paragraph form.

How's the Weather?

Read sentences to help you decide what the weather is like.

People are always talking about the weather. Read these quotations and tell what the weather is like. The first one is done for you.

1. "We can go skiing tomorrow."

   It's snowing.

2. "Look, a hat is flying down the street."

   _____

3. "I'm not taking my umbrella, but I am wearing my raincoat."

   _____

4. "The sky is gray and dark. You can't see the sun."

   _____

5. "I'm not wearing my coat today. My jacket is fine for this weather."

   _____

6. "Listen to me, Billy. You have to wear your gloves and hat and coat today."

   _____

7. "Look at the thermometer. It's 105°F. Wow!"

   _____

8. "Oh my goodness, you are wet all over. Your shoes and socks are wet too!"

   _____

9. "The bright light hurts my eyes. I have to wear my dark glasses."

   _____

10. "We can't play baseball today. The field is wet and muddy."

    _____

ⒹⒶⓉⒶ ⒷⒶⓃⓀ

cloudy	drizzling	pouring	snowing	warm
cold	hot	raining	sunny	windy

110 **Skill Objectives: Building vocabulary; making inferences.** Teach/review the weather vocabulary in the Data Bank. Do the first one or two examples orally as a group, then assign the page for independent work. Have students discuss their answers.

What and Why?

A. Write the letter for the "Why" that goes with each "What." The first one is done for you.

What are they doing?

1. __e__ Maria is buying two pairs of shoes.
2. ____ Angel is taking off his sweater.
3. ____ Dot is putting on her gloves.
4. ____ Francisco is putting on his raincoat.
5. ____ The nurses are putting on their uniforms.
6. ____ Loc is putting on his bathing suit.
7. ____ James and Sandy are wearing wedding rings.
8. ____ Pablo is putting on his boots.

Why are they doing it?

a. They are married.
b. Her hands are very cold.
c. He is going out in the rain.
d. They are going to work.
e. She is at a shoe sale.
f. It's hot in his room.
g. He is going out in the snow.
h. He is going to the beach.

B. What about you? Tell "why." Use complete sentences. The first one is done for you.

1. You are closing the window. *I am closing the window because it's cold.*
   _____

2. You are wearing sunglasses. _____
   _____

3. You are not going to school. _____
   _____

4. You are calling the fire department. _____
   _____

5. You are crying. _____
   _____

6. You are cleaning your room. _____
   _____

7. You are studying. _____
   _____

D A T A   B A N K

today is a holiday	my room is messy	it's cold	there is a fire down the street
I have a big test tomorrow	it's very sunny outside	my best friend is moving away

Skill Objective: Recognizing cause and effect. On the board, write the sentence, *Paul is taking off his hat.* Ask, "Why is he taking off his hat?" Let students suggest a variety of reasons: He is in a house/a church. It is very hot, etc. Repeat this cause-effect activity with the sentences, *I am running* and *Her hair is wet.* Encourage students to come up with a wide range of possible causes. Do the first few examples in Parts A and B together, then assign the page as independent work. Students may use the causes in the Data Bank for Part B or make up their own.

The Dinner Party

It is 7:55. The Smiths are coming to dinner at 8:00. Gina and Frank are not ready for the Smiths. They want everything to be perfect when the Smiths arrive. Mr. Smith is Frank's boss.

"Hurry, Frank, the Smiths are coming soon. We have to set the table. Bring in the dishes, please. I already have the bowls for the salad and the cups for the coffee. I don't have the knives, forks, and spoons. Bring those with the dishes.

I have to put the tablecloth on the table and find the good napkins. Hurry, Frank, there's so much to do!"

"I'm coming," says Frank. Frank is carrying the dishes, the knives, the forks, and the spoons. He and Gina begin to set the table. Everything is ready. It is 8:00. At 8:01, the Smiths knock on the door. Gina and Frank answer the door together. They are ready for their perfect evening.

A. Answer the following questions. Use short answers. The first one is done for you.

1. When are the Smiths coming to dinner? _____*8:00*_____

2. Who is Mr. Smith? _____

3. Are Gina and Frank ready for the Smiths at 7:55? _____

4. What do Gina and Frank have to do? _____

5. What does Frank have to bring? _____

6. What does Gina have already? _____

7. What does Gina have to put on the table? _____

8. What does she have to find? _____

9. What time is it when everything is ready? _____

10. When do the Smiths knock on the door? _____

B. What is the main idea of this story? Circle the best answer.

a. Frank's boss is coming.

b. Gina and Frank are having a perfect evening.

c. Frank and Gina are getting ready for a party.

d. Gina has to find the napkins.

C. Talk about these questions.

1. Why do Gina and Frank want everything to be perfect when the Smiths arrive?

2. Is Frank a good husband? Why or why not?

3. Do the Smiths come too early? Explain your answer.

Skill Objectives: Identifying main idea and details; making inferences and judgments. Read the story aloud as students follow along, or have a volunteer read it. Explain any new vocabulary. Have students reread the text silently, then answer the questions in Parts A and B. Correct Part A together. Then discuss why "getting ready for a party" is the only correct answer to Part B. Use the questions in Part C as springboards for class discussion.

Crossword Puzzle

Write the words in the right places. Number 1 Across and number 1 Down are done for you.

Across

1. Please ____ down.
4. Guitars make it.
7. Where you get books.
9. Person high up in a circus.
10. Where you sleep.
12. In winter, Gina ____ down the hills.
15. You eat in them.
18. Either this ____ that.
19. What ____ of shop is it?
21. Get ____ of here.
23. New and up to date.
26. Where did she ____?
27. Jim is ____ in the gym.
30. Where you play basketball.
32. The book is ____ the table.
33. Maria is ____ the book.
34. When it is ____, everything is white.

Down

1. Rosa is ____ at my house.
2. Where you probably are now (if you're in school).
3. A new ____ of shoes.
4. That's ____ pencil, not yours.
5. What ice cream and snow are.
6. They were ____ at pictures.
8. What is ____?
11. What happens in 15 across.
13. Have a ____ of coffee.
14. What are you ____ about?
16. You are studying and ____ am I.
17. ____ or false?
20. Will you ____ something for me?
21. Look at that boy ____ there!
22. At that place.
24. What are you ____ tonight?
25. Yes or ____?
28. Brother of a daughter.
29. It makes the car go.
31. Was it a ____ or a woman?

(Answers on page 127)

Skill Objectives: Understanding word definitions; using context clues. Be sure students understand how a crossword puzzle is constructed. Point out that 1 across and 1 down share the same initial "s." Do several clues across and down as a group. Help students note the number of letter spaces in the word and any letter clues provided. (For example, 9 across has seven letters, and the first letter is "a," provided by the answer to 1 down.) When you feel students are ready, have them complete the puzzle independently or working in pairs. Answers are on page 127.

113

Dear Dot

Dear Dot—

The Smiths are coming for dinner this Sunday. I like the Smiths, but they always talk about their health problems. They talk about their headaches and their backaches or stomach problems or sore throats. I don't like that kind of conversation, especially at the dinner table. I like to talk about movies, books, and the news. What can I do?

Healthy

1. Who is coming to dinner? _____

2. When are they coming to dinner? _____

3. What kind of health problems do they talk about? _____

_____

4. What does Healthy like to talk about? _____

_____

5. What is your advice for Healthy? Write a letter telling her what to do and what NOT to do.

Dear Healthy _____ ,

_____

_____

_____

_____

_____

_____

_____

_____

_____

_____

Skill Objectives: Reading comprehension; making judgments; writing a letter. Read the letter aloud as students follow along, or have a volunteer read it. Explain any unfamiliar words. Ask students to reread the letter silently, then answer questions 1-4. Discuss and correct their answers. Discuss possible answers to question 5, and then have students write their answers to Healthy.

Vocabulary Review

Complete each sentence with a word from the Data Bank.

1. My _____ name is Gonzalez.

2. Open your _____ to page twenty.

3. He is walking _____ the steps.

4. _____ I go to the bathroom, please.

5. I want to see the nurse; I feel _____ .

6. Mary is _____ blue shorts and a gray blouse.

7. Every country has its own _____ .

8. The bus _____ Barrington at 6:30 a.m.

9. My shoes are _____ the bed.

10. The library is _____ the bank and the post office.

11. Janet isn't chubby; she's _____ .

12. Your cousin is a _____ person.

13. _____ are sweet and round.

14. Mrs. Perez is buying a _____ of milk.

15. Mr. Yu is looking for his _____ .

16. Pat's _____ have blond hair.

17. Pablo is sleeping in the _____ .

18. Do you live on the _____ floor?

19. A _____ types letters in an office.

20. Dinh is _____ ; he comes from Vietnam.

D A T A B A N K

grapes	first	up	leaves	between	wife	wearing	last
thin	secretary		under	Vietnamese		sisters	May
friendly		bedroom	book	sick		flag	gallon

Vocabulary Review. The following eight pages present a cumulative review of key vocabulary used in *Skill Sharpeners 1*. Familiar formats are used so that students can work independently on these pages.

115

Vocabulary Review

Complete each sentence with a word from the Data Bank.

1. They are _____ their car to Chicago.

2. The _____ says No Right Turn.

3. I have a _____ throat.

4. I am _____ tennis with my brother.

5. On _____ I'm going to the library.

6. Don't move; the photographer is taking a _____ .

7. _____ your hand to answer a question.

8. Nurses take _____ of sick people.

9. Do you know your address and _____ code?

10. The _____ in the spring is rainy and warm.

11. He is _____ for fruits and vegetables.

12. _____ are many banks in this city.

13. Her first _____ is Debbie.

14. A pilot flies _____ .

15. _____ like to play with toys and games.

16. My birthday is on the _____ of this month.

17. Please _____ the dog if he is hungry.

18. The girls are _____ television in the living room.

19. _____ many people are in your school?

20. Mary's _____ is $45,000.00 a year.

DATA BANK

feed	name	care	Children	driving	weather	airplanes
salary	shopping		Wednesday	sign	watching	There
How	sore	Raise	tenth	playing	zip	picture

116

Vocabulary Review

Complete each sentence with a word from the Data Bank.

1. Please _____ the blackboard.

2. Jane doesn't understand the story; she's _____ .

3. I have a _____ of boots in the bedroom.

4. Four _____ equal one dollar.

5. The bus _____ at Plymouth at 4:15.

6. Most basketball players are _____ .

7. I would like a chicken _____ , please.

8. She's not very _____ today; she only wants a salad.

9. Carl is buying a _____ of bread at the store.

10. Susan's _____ is a nice man.

11. There are 10 males and 14 _____ in our class.

12. My keys are upstairs in Bill's _____ .

13. The boys are _____ magazines in the library.

14. Mary and her father are washing the car out in the _____ .

15. The _____ look and dress the same.

16. The _____ clean the school building every day.

17. What's your _____ color?

18. My _____ hurt when I walk too much.

19. Two students are _____ in the home economics class.

20. That store is always _____ on Saturday mornings.

🄳🄰🅃🄰 🄱🄰🄽🄺

brother-in-law	twins	erase	hungry	custodians	cooking
quarters	tall	females	apartment	reading	arrives
loaf	yard	favorite	confused	feet	pair	crowded	sandwich

Vocabulary Review

Complete each sentence with a word from the Data Bank.

1. Mae Lee is going to the doctor _____ work.

2. Sandra has to take care of the _____ this afternoon.

3. Clean the sink and the _____ , please.

4. My girlfriend is a very _____ girl.

5. I don't know the answer to those arithmetic _____ .

6. Maine is one of the New England _____ .

7. Andrea is wearing her favorite _____ .

8. My favorite breakfast is ham and _____ .

9. The door is locked and I don't have the _____ .

10. I'm not sick today; I feel _____ .

11. Chess is a difficult _____ to learn.

12. I have to _____ ; my mother is waiting for me.

13. The boys are late; they have to _____ to school.

14. My friends are cooking dinner in the _____ .

15. Please don't talk; you are in a _____ .

16. Paula's _____ are in the closet.

17. The receptionists have to _____ coffee for the customers.

18. The boys are buying two rock and roll _____ .

19. Maria is staying in Los Angeles for one _____ .

20. It's hot in here; open the _____ .

D A T A   B A N K

library	fine	after	pants	game	dress
key	kitchen	window	go	make	baby
bathtub	week	problems	eggs	records	states

beautiful · run

Vocabulary Review

Complete each sentence with a word from the Data Bank.

1. Raul isn't walking to school today; he's taking the _____.

2. Don't touch that wall; the paint is _____.

3. I have to wear a _____; these pants are too big.

4. The teacher is _____ because the students are cheating.

5. Mrs. Pena's office is on the third floor of the Tower _____.

6. My plane is _____ soon; I have to say good-bye.

7. They drink _____ at breakfast every morning.

8. His _____ is an excellent athlete.

9. What _____ shoe are you looking for?

10. My hands are cold; where are my _____?

11. The steak is very _____ at this restaurant.

12. I am _____; may I have a drink?

13. In the winter we can _____ on this pond.

14. In the summer, _____ is everyone's favorite dessert.

15. Turn on the _____; I can't see a thing.

16. Mario is home alone; his _____ are away for the day.

17. The _____ is talking to the airport manager.

18. There are a lot of _____ in the store today.

19. I can't eat a large pizza; I want a _____ one, please.

20. I have to go to the dentist; I have a bad _____.

DATA BANK

ice cream	tooth	coffee	bus	lamp	angry
size	pilot	daughter	belt	parents	people	gloves
thirsty	wet	Building	small	skate	leaving	expensive

Vocabulary Review

Put the words from the Data Bank into the correct boxes.

Body Parts

1. _____
2. _____
3. _____
4. _____
5. _____

Fruit

1. _____
2. _____
3. _____
4. _____
5. _____

Occupations

1. _____
2. _____
3. _____
4. _____
5. _____

Clothing

1. _____
2. _____
3. _____
4. _____
5. _____

Parts of a Bicycle

1. _____
2. _____
3. _____
4. _____
5. _____

Family Members

1. _____
2. _____
3. _____
4. _____
5. _____

Time Words

1. _____
2. _____
3. _____
4. _____
5. _____

Colors

1. _____
2. _____
3. _____
4. _____
5. _____

D A T A B A N K

afternoon	boots	granddaughter	night	son
ankle	chain	grapes	noon	strawberries
apple	chef	gray	pear	suit
architect	chest	handlebars	pedal	throat
aunt	coat	jeans	purple	thumb
banana	cousin	knee	red	tire
bathrobe	engineer	lawyer	seat	waitress
black	evening	morning	sister	yellow

Vocabulary Review. See annotation on page 115.

Vocabulary Review

Put the words from the Data Bank into the correct boxes.

Parts of a Car	Animals	Weather Words
1. _____	1. _____	1. _____
2. _____	2. _____	2. _____
3. _____	3. _____	3. _____
4. _____	4. _____	4. _____
5. _____	5. _____	5. _____

Furniture	Vegetables	Rooms
1. _____	1. _____	1. _____
2. _____	2. _____	2. _____
3. _____	3. _____	3. _____
4. _____	4. _____	4. _____
5. _____	5. _____	5. _____

Ordinal Numbers	Eating Utensils
1. _____	1. _____
2. _____	2. _____
3. _____	3. _____
4. _____	4. _____
5. _____	5. _____

D A T A   B A N K

armchair	car	elephant	kitchen	steering wheel
bathroom	cold	fifth	knife	sunny
beans	corn	first	living room	table
bed	cucumber	fork	plate	third
bedroom	cup	fourth	potatoes	tiger
bookcase	dining room	headlight	second	warm
brake pedal	dog	horse	sofa	windshield wiper
carrots	drizzling	ignition	spoon	windy

Vocabulary Review

A. Match the words in column A with their definitions in column B.

Column A

1. astronaut _____
2. Canadian _____
3. restaurant _____
4. avenue _____
5. dialing _____
6. beach _____
7. suitcase _____
8. messy _____
9. thirsty _____
10. fix _____
11. throat _____
12. drizzling _____
13. behind _____
14. single _____
15. poor _____
16. son _____
17. sink _____
18. veterinarian _____
19. university _____
20. mice _____

Column B

a. street or road
b. dirty, not clean
c. place to swim
d. not married
e. repair, make better
f. doctor for animals
g. front part of neck
h. in back of
i. place to eat breakfast, lunch, or dinner
j. not rich, without money
k. place to wash
l. man or woman in space
m. school or college
n. small animals with long tails
o. male child
p. calling a phone number
q. raining a little
r. person from Canada
s. wanting a drink
t. kind of case for carrying clothes

B. Now show that you know what the words mean. Write a complete sentence for each word in column A. Underline the word you are using. Example: Maria is packing her <u>suitcase</u>.

Vocabulary Review. See annotation on page 115.

End of Book Test: Completing Familiar Structures

Circle the best answer.

Example: _____ you going to go to the bank today?

a. Is   (b. Are)   c. Do   d. Can

1. Liana is here but her sisters _____.

a. can't   b. isn't   c. don't   d. aren't

2. Bob is _____.

a. an architect   b. one architect   c. architect   d. architects

3. Francis is living _____ Main Street.

a. to   b. at   c. on   d. for

4. My brother is listening _____ the news.

a. to   b. at   c. on   d. for

5. Your socks are _____ the bed.

a. across from   b. over   c. under   d. next

6. Mr. and Mrs. Jackson _____ the newspaper now.

a. reading   b. read   c. reads   d. are reading

7. _____ bananas are very good.

a. These   b. This   c. That   d. Them

8. _____ one hospital in Boxville.

a. It is   b. There is   c. It has   d. There are

9. Juanita can swim but her brother _____.

a. isn't   b. don't   c. doesn't   d. can't

10. What's the weather like today? It's _____.

a. rain   b. to rain   c. raining   d. rains

11. That's John's coat. Please give it to _____.

a. him   b. his   c. he   d. himself

12. _____'s a sale at Filene's today.

a. Their   b. The   c. There   d. It

End of Book Test. The following testing pages will help you evaluate each student's strengths and weaknesses, and indicate his or her readiness to proceed to the next level of instruction. Review directions and examples with the class, then assign the pages as independent work. Remind students to try each answer choice in the blank space to determine which choice is correct.

123

End of Book Test: Completing Familiar Structures (Continued)

Circle the best answer.

13. _____ is she coming?

    a. Where   b. When   c. Who   d. What

14. Why can't Paula come to class? She _____ a bad headache.

    a. has   b. have   c. is   d. having

15. Our vacation is _____ August.

    a. on   b. at   c. for   d. in

16. _____ are they going to do tonight?

    a. What   b. Where   c. What time   d. Why

17. There's an old church _____ the library.

    a. next   b. in front   c. across   d. near

18. Bob and Jill are tired, so I am helping _____.

    a. they   b. them   c. there   d. their

19. Is this your coat? No, it's _____ coat.

    a. Mary   b. Marys   c. hers   d. Mary's

20. What are you _____?

    a. eat   b. to eat   c. eating   d. eats

21. How much _____ those boots?

    a. are   b. is   c. do cost   d. does

22. _____ umbrella is this?

    a. Who's   b. How's   c. What's   d. Whose

23. How _____ airports are there in Dallas?

    a. many   b. much   c. are   d. are there

24. I am looking _____ a new pair of shoes.

    a. from   b. in   c. for   d. on

25. Can you help me? No, I'm sorry. I _____ go to the dentist.

    a. have   b. am   c. going   d. have to

End of Book Test. See annotation on page 123.

End of Book Test: Writing Questions

Read the sentence. Write the question.

Example: Linda is taking piano lessons at the conservatory.

Where _____ *is Linda taking piano lessons* _____ ?

1. Mario is going to the library at ten o'clock.

   When _____ ?

2. They are traveling in Central America now.

   Where _____ ?

3. Carlotta is wearing her sister's sweater.

   What _____ ?

4. The maid is cleaning the room.

   Who _____ ?

5. There are four students from Vietnam in my class.

   How many _____ ?

6. No, I'm not happy with my new apartment.

   Are _____ ?

7. Carlos is playing volleyball in the park.

   Where _____ ?

8. That car is $10,000.

   How much _____ ?

9. It's going to rain tonight.

   What _____ ?

10. She's crying because she is sad.

    Why _____ ?

11. I'm wearing my brother's sneakers.

    Whose _____ ?

12. No, Nancy's mother is an engineer.

    Is _____ ?

End of Book Test: Reading for Details

The Mural

Mrs. Cabral's class is working hard. They are painting a mural outside. A mural is a large picture on a wall. The students are painting their mural on one of the school walls. They are painting a picture of Waverly Street, the main street in their town.

Carlos is painting the buildings. He is painting the bank now. It is between the post office and the supermarket. Rosa and Anh are painting the people. Rosa is working on a picture of Officer Collins, the policeman. Anh is painting a group of schoolchildren. They are playing soccer. Freddy can paint clouds well. He is painting the sky.

Some other students are painting cars, trees, birds, flowers, and houses. They are using bright, pretty colors. Van's favorite color is red. He is painting everything red. There is a red airplane and a red cat in the picture already. The students have to stop Van soon. They want their mural to be beautiful, not funny.

Answer the following questions.

1. What is a mural? _____

2. Where are the students painting the mural? _____

3. What are the students painting a picture of? _____

4. Where is the bank? _____

5. Who is Rosa painting? _____

6. Who is Anh painting? _____

7. What can Freddy paint well? _____

8. What are the other students painting? _____

9. What is Van's favorite color? _____

10. Why do the students have to stop Van? _____

End of Book Test. Students should read this story several times, then answer the comprehension questions. Accept factually correct short answers as well as complete sentences.

Sample Paragraph

Use this as a sample of the way to write a paragraph.

Title of the paragraph → *The Apartment*

> *Mary's apartment is a beautiful place. It is on the fourth floor of a tall building. The apartment has one bedroom, a kitchen, a bathroom, and a living room. Each room is clean and neat. Mary's favorite room is the living room. When Mary comes home from work, she likes to sit at the window and watch the boats sail down the river. Watching the boats helps her to relax after a hard day at the office.*

All sentences begin with capital letters.

All sentences end with a period.

The first word in a paragraph is indented, that is, it starts a few spaces in from the margin.

Each paragraph starts on a new line.

Answer to puzzle on page 113

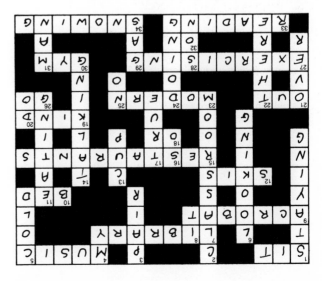

Sample Paragraph. Use this page as a sample for the task of writing a paragraph. References are made to it on many pages that include instructions to write paragraphs. You may wish to point out that not all paragraphs require titles, and that all should contain a topic sentence; this is usually, but not always, the first sentence in the paragraph.

127

Skills Index

The pages listed below are those on which the skills are introduced and/or emphasized. Many of the skills appear. incidentally, on other pages as well.

Grammatical/Structural Skills

Adjectives, 44, 45
  a and *an*, 58
  possessive adjectives, 9, 44
Nouns
  plurals, 82
  possessives ('s), 95
Prepositions, 37, 38, 64
Pronouns, 44, 53, 95
There is/are, 81, 84, 85
Verbs
  future form: *going to,* 94, 96, 97, 98
  have to, has to, 100
  modals: *can, can't,* 101, 102
  present forms of "to be," 43, 45, 70
  present progressive, 53, 66, 67, 68, 70, 83
  simple present, 72, 73
    uses of *like,* 59

Pronunciation

Mr., Mrs., Ms., 63

Reading Comprehension Skills

Classifying, 30, 55, 57, 65
Drawing conclusions, 96, 100
Fact *vs.* opinion, 88
Following directions, 11, 12, 13, 39, 40, 41
Identifying main idea and details, 32, 34, 39, 50, 89, 97, 98, 112
Identifying topic, 88, 89
Making inferences, 47, 56, 74, 89, 104, 110, 112
Making judgments, 51, 60, 71, 80, 91, 99, 107, 112, 114
Reading a biography, 47
Reading for details, 78, 87
Recognizing cause and effect, 111
Sequencing, 21, 90, 109
Using context clues, 31, 113

Reading in the Content Areas

Math
  money, prices, and problems, 28, 29, 54, 75
  number names and counting, 16, 81
  ordinal numbers, 21, 22
  time zone math problems, 93
  telling time, 17, 18, 35, 36, 92
Social Studies
  city maps, 40, 41
  community places, 40, 41, 81, 94
  countries and nationalities, 34, 46, 77, 79
  occupations, 15, 72, 73, 74, 75, 78
  U.S. cities and states, 87, 88, 89, 96, 97

Study Skills

Getting information from graphics
  bar graph, 75
  calendar, 21, 22
  circle chart, 86
  diagrams, 62, 68, 85, 103, 104
  family tree, 61, 62
  library card and address form, 10
  maps, 14, 40, 41, 42
  menu, 54
  road signs, 105, 106
  time table, 36
Interviewing, 76, 84, 102
Labeling diagrams, 14, 108
Making charts, 34, 56
Plotting information on maps and charts, 20, 41, 62, 85, 86, 102
Test-taking skills
  multiple choice, 25, 42, 52, 56, 68
  cloze, 69

Vocabulary Development

Body parts, 108, 109
Clothes, 26, 27
Community places, 40, 41
Countries and nationalities, 34, 77
Days of the week, months, 20, 21, 22
Family members, 61, 62
Feelings, 24, 51, 54, 60, 71, 80, 91, 99, 107, 114
Food, 52, 54, 55, 56, 57
Musical instruments, 101
Occupations, 15, 72, 73, 78
Parts of a bike and car, 103, 104
Rooms and furniture, 17, 65, 68
School vocabulary, 11, 12, 13, 14, 15, 83, 84
Seasons, 32
Sports and games, 30, 101
Telephone, 90
Traffic terms, 105, 106
Weather terms, 32, 110

Writing Skills

Autobiographical paragraphs, 50, 90, 101
Descriptions, 24, 27, 44, 49
Descriptive paragraphs, 37, 42, 47, 76, 83
Friendly letters, 49, 99, 107, 114
Informative essays, 79
Negative statements, 81, 85
Paragraph, sample, 127
Questions, 33, 46, 61, 70, 96
Rules for capitalization, 48
Spelling, 67, 82